RAINBOW BRIDGE

A True Story about Rescue Cats

Susan Cilyk

ATHENA PRESS
LONDON

RAINBOW BRIDGE
A True Story about Rescue Cats
Copyright © Susan Cilyk 2004

All Rights Reserved

ISBN 1 84401 270 0

First Published 2004 by
ATHENA PRESS
Queen's House, 2 Holly Road
Twickenham, TW1 4EG
United Kingdom

Printed for Athena Press

RAINBOW BRIDGE
A True Story about Rescue Cats

*My thanks to Pat, Sue, Hilary, Val and Bobby
for their help and encouragement,
and to all the cats for their inspiration.*

Preface

'Just this side of heaven is a place called Rainbow Bridge. When an animal dies that has been especially close to someone here, that pet goes to Rainbow Bridge. There are meadows and hills for all our special friends so they can run and play together. There is plenty of food and water and sunshine, and our friends are warm and comfortable. All the animals who had been ill and old are restored to health and vigour; those who were hurt or maimed are made whole and strong again, just as we remember them in our dreams of days and times gone by.

'The animals are happy and content, except for one small thing: they miss someone very special to them who had to be left behind. They all run and play together, but the day comes when one suddenly stops and looks into the distance. The bright eyes are intent; the eager body quivers. Suddenly he begins to break away from the group, flying over the green grass, his legs carrying him faster and faster.

'*You* have been spotted, and when you and your special friend finally meet, you cling together in joyous reunion, never to be parted again. The happy kisses rain upon your face; your hands again caress the beloved head, and you look once more into the trusting eyes of your beloved pet, so long gone from your life but never absent from your heart.

'Then you cross the Rainbow Bridge together...'

Anon.

First seen published in *The Cat* magazine, the official journal of Cats Protection (previously known as The Cats Protection League), registered charity number 203644.

Contents

Chapter One
The Beginning

A S I STOOD IN A PRIVATE CAR PARK ON AN ABNORMALLY cold Sunday afternoon in early summer setting a trap with pilchards, my thoughts were filled with images of the many times I had been in similar positions...

The trap would cause no harm to the cat I was trying to catch other than the immediate fright of being caught in the first place. The object of my attention on this occasion was a sweet little tabby-and-white cat called Katy. She was heavily pregnant and I had been trying to catch her for a week. Katy was not the sort of cat that you could just pick up and cuddle; she liked the company of humans just so long as they kept their distance, and she had obviously been highly amused and entertained by my feeble attempts to catch her during the course of the previous week.

Katy and I had become friends of a sort in a short space of time, but not all the cats I had known over the past fifteen years had been so eager to become acquainted with me...

While I waited in the car for Katy to arrive I tried to remember when my love for cats had turned into a passion, and I began to recall the cats that had shared my life and my home, and the countless others who had touched my life for just a few minutes or hours... Strangely enough, it had all started with a mouse.

My first ever cat was a beautiful tortie-tabby called Tabatha (and that was the way in which her name was spelt – I wanted a singular name for a special cat). I was living in a bedsit in Brixton, south-east London at the time, and although I desperately wanted a cat it wasn't until I saw a mouse scampering across my kitchen floor that I pleaded with the landlady (who lived on the premises and was an animal lover herself) to let me have one. I was then – and still am – petrified of mice, alive or dead. When I consider my ample frame I appreciate that the mice who have entered my life are probably far more frightened of me, but I don't like their tails, their feet and the speed with which they move. However, I still wish that the feline population were not so cruel to them and did not see them as the cat equivalent of a takeaway pizza!

I was going on holiday for a week to Majorca, and on the way to the airport my companion and I stopped off at the RSPCA sanctuary. There in a pen was Tabatha, and as we looked at her through the glass, her paw came up to try and touch us through the barrier. They would not reserve her for a week, so I had to leave her behind and spent a week of lovely warmth and sunshine wishing I were back home.

At that time I was not a confident driver and I had a beaten-up old Mini Clubman, which, if I am truthful, frightened me to death. I used to have nightmares about travelling along the road with pieces of the car falling off until I ended up like Fred Flintstone, running along the ground while holding the chassis of the car around me.

However, my determination to have a cat surpassed all those fears, and I set off on the Saturday morning to see if the cat (or kitten, as she was really) was still there. I wasn't sure of the route and I hit fog so dense I couldn't even see the road markings or signs until I was on them, and then I didn't have enough time to read them. The whole world had taken on an eerie, silent feel, and I finally lost my way totally. As I went along a road, the fog lifted for a moment and at last I could see a sign with a place name that I recognised: 'LONDON 7 MILES'.

I gave up and made my way back home again, where I had a quick coffee before bravely setting out once more having checked the map for the hundredth time. This time my determination paid off and I had more luck. The fog had lifted so I was able to see where I was going, although I still fell on the sanctuary by sheer luck rather than finding it through any real navigational skills.

Joy, oh joy! Tabatha was still there, and the formalities over, into a pet-carrying box she went and home she came. She almost demolished the box in the car on the journey back home, but I managed to get her indoors without losing her, and she rushed about my tiny bedsit in sheer excitement at the comparative freedom she had suddenly acquired.

Tabatha quickly became the darling of the household – including the landlady's son and their other lodger. She had a favourite toy which was a spinning top – like the ones you get in a Christmas cracker – which she carried everywhere with her. If you met her on the stairs, you were meant to throw the top either up- or downstairs for her to rush after, retrieve and drop at your feet so you could play the game over and over again. I often heard the voices of the other occupants of the house on the landing: 'Do you want me to throw it for you? Which way will it go, up or down?' This would be followed by praise for her intelligence and then the whole charade would start again until one or the other got bored – usually it was Tabatha!

Another of her little tricks was to 'hide' on the landing, and as someone walked up the stairs she would either jump on their shoulders or pat their head through the railings. I can assure you that this gave everyone in the house a fright from time to time – imagine having something land on you from out of the darkness!

After her first year with me, it was time to move house and start at the bottom of the housing ladder, so a property had to be found with a garden! We finally moved into a first-floor maisonette with its own front door and garden. Tabatha had never been out, so I gradually had to introduce her to the big world that existed beyond her front door. She stayed in when I was at work and had her fun in the evenings between me coming home and bedtime. During the period of confinement indoors during the daytime she became an expert on the comings and goings in the road. My neighbour, Jean, told me one day that Tabatha spent most of her day sitting on the windowsill watching the world go by; she would watch Jean as she came out of her gate to go to the shops and she would still be watching as Jean walked down the road past our maisonette. When Jean got to the corner, she couldn't stop herself from looking back towards my window – only to find Tabatha still watching her.

'I can't resist a quick wave when I get to the corner!' said our kind neighbour.

Although we lived in a quiet road, there was a main road nearby and we were forever hearing the sound of screeching brakes and the crash of metal as cars collided on the junction. One Sunday evening I was watching television while Tabatha was asleep in the chair next to me. All of a sudden our peace was shattered by a loud noise outside – another car crash. I leapt to my feet and went to have a look. Poking my head around the closed curtains I was astonished to meet Tabatha's eyes as she poked her head around the curtains at the other end of the window: we'd both decided this was one noise that needed investigating.

During the summer months Tabatha thought that there were occasions when she was old enough and brave enough to stay out on her own, even if Mum had to go to work. On these occasions I would make absolutely sure that I was home on time, and on one such evening when I opened the gate I heard a plaintiff little *Meow!* coming from one of the lime trees in the front garden. As I looked up I could see Tabatha staring down at me from amongst the leaves; my precious cat had probably been chased up there by the old black tom we had noticed outside our door on several occasions recently. I don't know how long she had been imitating a leaf for on that day, but she was so relieved to see me – and had such trust in me – that as she made her way down she suddenly decided to let go of the bark of the tree and just fell in the hopes that I would catch her. I did, of course! Tabatha became quite proficient at climbing up and down that tree during the course of her life as she attempted to keep out of the way of any marauding tom or unfriendly female cat.

The maisonette downstairs went up for sale and at the same time a friend of mine from work was looking for somewhere to buy, so I put vendor and purchaser together and Aunty Pat moved in as our neighbour after a few months. By now Tabatha was quite independent and spent most of the summer outside. Sometimes Aunty Pat would get home first and give this starving cat a nice tasty piece of chicken to keep her going until Mum came home. Uncle Fred and Aunty Jean, who lived in the house next door, also took pity on Tabatha on occasions – especially when they saw her trying to catch her own dinner, which was Tabatha's party piece.

Jean would often throw a bit of bread out of the window and onto the lawn for the birds to eat. Tabatha would see this and wait under a bush in their garden. As a bird landed on the grass to eat the bread the whole bush would begin to move as Tabatha wriggled her bottom ready to spring, and at the same time a tail would appear at the top of the bush and this would wave frantically in the air. The birds could also see all this activity, and taking a last piece of bread, they would fly up and out of harm's way. A few seconds or maybe minutes later, Tabatha would suddenly 'fly' out from under the bush and sit with her nose against the piece of bread waiting for the birds to come back. Needless to say, they never did. In fact, I never, ever saw Tabatha catch a bird in the entire fifteen years of her life with me.

When Tabatha was outside, having no cat flap at the time, she would howl at the front door and paw at the letterbox to alert me to the fact the she needed to come in. There were three steps inside the front door that led up into the living space, and one evening, having opened the door for her to come in, I shut the door, turned around and there on the top step was a mouse that, unnoticed by me, Tabatha had obviously been carrying in her mouth. And there she was, proudly sitting next to it anticipating praise for her hunting skills. Panic set in immediately: I screamed and the mouse rushed into the kitchen that was then undergoing major refurbishment. The mouse disappeared, but where was it – had it gone down the gap between the floor and the wall? Being brave, and this being the 1970s, I found a pair of my highest platform shoes to put on and then tied my clothes up around my waist. (Remember that my passion for cats did not extend to mice!) I rang the maisonette downstairs to ask Pat for advice. She came up to survey the scene and devised a brilliant idea: sprinkle talcum powder around all the gaps in the skirting and then when the mouse came out I would see its footprints in the powder. So we set-to liberally sprinkling powder all round the kitchen, but there was one major flaw to her plan: she didn't tell me what to do if I *did* see footprints, and it didn't occur to me at the time to ask her. I went to bed stuffing all manner of things under the door so that the mouse could not creep up on me in the night! I rushed out to work the next day and met Pat at the railway station.

'Did you look for footprints?' she asked.

I replied that I hadn't had time but would look tonight. Actually, I was too scared to look – I admit!

That evening, when Pat arrived home, she found a lost

soul sitting on the stone staircase leading up to my front door with a cat who was totally bemused as to why her mother would not open the front door and get her tea. Dropping her shopping in her own hallway, Pat came up with me to see whether the mouse had left its footprints in the powder: nothing.

I spent a very jumpy few hours in platform shoes until the telephone rang late in the evening. It was Pat, just making sure that I was still alive and hadn't been eaten by a mouse.

'That's really nice of you,' I said and continued, 'I haven't seen any sign of movement in the powder and I have checked it myself this evening.'

Pat then went on: 'I'm not surprised that you haven't seen it – it has just run across my curtain rail! What shall I do?'

'Ring Fred,' was my response.

The telephone rang in the house next door and Uncle Fred was appraised of the dilemma his two 'girls next door' had found themselves in. On went his shoes and round he came to Pat's flat while I waited upstairs in mine. Search as he might there was no sign of the mouse, so Aunty Pat spent an equally miserable night sharing her home with an unwanted guest. We guessed that the mouse had entered her flat via the gap in the skirting at one end of my kitchen and then gone into a cupboard in her flat that lay directly beneath it. The cupboard doors were louvered so the mouse would have had no difficulty getting out of the cupboard. From there it must have climbed down one of the wooden support posts and into her flat.

'I thought he was probably hungry so I left a pile of dried mixed fruit on the kitchen floor overnight,' said my brave friend.

The next day was Friday, and rather than spend a night indoors waiting to be attacked we both decided to go and watch the sports at Crystal Palace. Neither of us had shown any interest before, but it seemed like a good idea that night.

A friend of mine, Ted, had been away and I rather hoped that he might turn up that night and rescue us fair maidens. He arrived while we were at the games, and Fred appraised him of what had happened. Ted, ever the gentleman, came out in search of us and found us in the fish and chip shop – he had a feeling that neither of us would have eaten anything, so he had a pretty shrewd idea of where we'd be.

He went indoors with Pat and I listened to the shouts and thuds from downstairs whilst remaining within the safety of my own walls, confident by now that I did not have a lodger. Eventually Ted caught the mouse and released it outside – well away from Tabatha's eyes.

Several nights later Tabatha tried the same trick again, but this time the mouse only got onto the threshold of the door. Next to the door was the cupboard where I kept my hoover so, one eye on the mouse, I reached for the hoover attachments and banged the floor just near the mouse. The mouse looked at me and then at Tabatha before scuttling back over the threshold of the door and outside once more: he obviously thought his chances of survival were greater with the cat. Pat had bravely listened to all the goings on from her own flat and admitted later that she had kept a very low profile in case she had been called in to do mouse rescue again.

Tabatha and I moved house again – not very far; we bought the house that Fred lived in and he and Jean went off to live in Surrey. Tabatha gave a glance back over her shoulder as she packed her toys and moved next door.

Soon after we were joined by more and more cats, all of which Tabatha took in her stride until she had to go to Cat Heaven at the grand old age of over fifteen and a half years.

Chapter Two

A Cat, Two Kittens and a Hurricane

ALTHOUGH I WAS UNAWARE OF IT AT THE TIME, MY destiny was already becoming obvious, and the much-loved and very spoilt Tabatha, who was now about eleven years old, found herself sharing me with other feline visitors.

During the late summer one year I noticed a tabby cat eating the food I put out for the birds, and so I started putting out some leftover cat food for her and she then began coming regularly for food having first sussed me out as a soft touch!

One day as I looked for her at the back door I noticed that she was not alone. With her, hiding in the undergrowth, were two tiny kittens, one black and white and the other white with tabby patches. I put the bowl of food down and tried to encourage the kittens to come and eat, but they were too cautious and retreated further into the undergrowth, waiting for me to go back indoors before joining their mother to eat from the bowl on the patio. I was no expert but I guessed that they were only about six weeks old, as they still appeared to have big blue eyes and were somewhat unsteady on their legs.

Our twice daily feeding sessions continued for a few weeks, but I still could not get anywhere near the kittens, who appeared to be growing rapidly. They took up residence in the greenhouse at night, and this was just as well because an unexpected hurricane hit in October 1987, and my first thoughts were for the safety of the cat and her kittens. I looked out of the back window to survey the scene of devastation in the garden and I could just make out three shapes in the greenhouse. Thankfully the dilapidated greenhouse had survived the initial battering from the hurricane-force winds that had howled and battered the environment for a large part of the night. The cat and kittens were safe and well. I prepared some food and took it to the back door. The mother cat ran to greet me, but as she did so her kittens followed her. She realised just in time and, scolding them, she chased them back to the comparative safety of the greenhouse. Once again she tried to get to the food and once again she had to chase the kittens back to their haven. By the third attempt the kittens seemed to have got the gist of what their mother wanted from them and she was able to rush over to the bowl, lift some food in her mouth and carry it back to the kittens in the greenhouse. I watched this happen two or three times until I could bear it no longer, and amid flying tree debris, howling winds and beating rain I left the safety of the house and took the food bowl down to the greenhouse.

The little family spent the entire day in the greenhouse, and I kept a watchful eye on them from the window. The kittens demolished the inside of the greenhouse that day, but they provided me with hours of entertainment at the same time. There was green netting on the inside of the greenhouse roof which hung down the side windows. The kittens managed to get inside the lower edge of the netting and climbed up as high as they could go. Although their combined weight couldn't have been more than a few pounds, it proved too much for the nails tacking the netting in place and they eventually gave way, leaving the two kittens clinging on by tiny, sharp claws while the netting swung from side to side. This was great fun: their own private swing! The game lasted for a few hours until the netting finally separated from the last few nails that held it to the roof of the greenhouse and kittens and netting fell into a heap on the greenhouse floor.

Gradually I was able to grab hold of the struggling, hissing little kittens, and although they were still very nervous, they soon decided to come and explore the inside of the house. Mumsie, as I had called the mother cat, had obviously decided that I was a suitable adoptive parent for her kittens, because she suddenly disappeared one day, leaving me in charge of her two tearaways. By now their names were Topsy and Twinkle, and with me to worry about them they hardly seemed to notice that their mother had gone. I was now the provider of food and all other necessities and so they became permanent fixtures in my home.

After a little time had passed one of my neighbours came down to see me.

'Sue, you've got cats, can you help? A cat has had four kittens in our garage and we don't know what to do.'

Following a brief question and answer session I knew that the mother cat had to be Mumsie, so armed with a cat basket I went with my neighbour to retrieve the kittens in the certain knowledge that if I went back with food I would also be able to catch Mumsie, and such was the case. The cat and her next litter of four kittens became the first of many occupants of my utility room.

I hadn't really had time to think about what I would do with my new lodgers; someone suggested that I ring the Cats Protection League, a registered charity that specialised in rescuing, neutering and re-homing stray and unwanted cats and kittens. I called the contact number and explained my dilemma, but the promised help never arrived and the kittens were getting bigger and more adventurous. Someone else knew a lady who did independent rescue work, and after a few phone calls cat and kittens were taken to her and all of them were eventually re-homed.

Topsy and Twinkle were now of an age to be spayed, and when I saw the old black stray that plagued my life mounting Twinkle outside my porch I resolved that this would have to be done immediately otherwise I would have another basket full of kittens to deal with.

The operations over, Topsy and Twinkle were confined indoors until they had recovered, and that's where they remained. Of course they were eventually allowed to come and go at will, and they were the first of many to discover that it was much quicker to howl at me to open the window for them to go out or come in than it was to wait for me to get around to opening the front door.

I learned very quickly that Topsy in particular had two types of meow. The first would be a plain old howl to say, 'Let me in – it's wet out here,' but the other howl was quite different and would alert me to the fact that care was needed before opening the window too far as she was bound to have something in her mouth. The prey could have been anything from a newt out of the pond to either a bird or a mouse.

'Topsy, you can come in but you must leave your friend outside,' I would say as I closed the window leaving her outside. I would make periodical checks through the glass to see whether she was still waiting and whether her mouth was empty. Both cats were hunters in the truest form – their mother had taught them to look after themselves if I should fail in my parental duties. I had a pond in the garden with five goldfish; I watched Twinkle one summer as she sat by the pond. She would wait until the fish basked in shallow water in the sunshine and then she would quickly flip them out with her paw. Despite all my attempts to make the pond cat proof the temptation to demonstrate her hunting prowess proved too much for her, and she managed to bypass all my tricks and the netting. By the end of the week there were no more goldfish in my pond. Then it was the turn of the newts, but these at least, being amphibians, stood a chance of scuttling under the heathers and out of the way of sharp claws and furry paws.

Twinkle developed a liking for coffee, be it in a mug with milk or just plain granules. If I left a mug of coffee in any state of preparation on its own for a few seconds I would come back to find Twinkle's head inside it – she still does this today. She was also accident prone; never an accurate jumper, one leap from Twinkle and the whole world appeared to collapse as mugs, plates and any other mobile item flew through the air. Very often she landed on the floor surrounded by crockery – all broken, of course – not on the surface she had intended to reach.

Topsy disappeared one day. She had gone out on the Saturday night and did not come in when I called her. This didn't distress me too much as they often had a night on the tiles if they were too busy plaguing some poor mouse or it was just too hot to be indoors at night. But when she did not appear on Sunday morning for breakfast I began to panic, just a little. I told all the neighbours and put up some notices asking people to check their sheds and garages and I went out to look – especially at the nearby main road: had she been run over? There was no sign of her. I continued my hunting vigil that night and for the next couple of nights when it was dark in the hopes that I would hear her call, but there was nothing. On the morning of the fourth day I heard a weak little meow from the other side of the front door, and there she was. I could see her through the glass. She rushed indoors, meowing as she went, and ran straight for the food bowls where she had quite a feast before falling asleep in one of the armchairs. Throughout the day she would wake up crying and I would go over to her, stroke her and remind her that she was home now and safe, whereupon she would fall back into another fitful sleep. I can only imagine that she had been shut in somewhere as she appeared a little dirty, hungry and very scared, but otherwise she had nothing wrong with her.

Topsy sadly passed away unexpectedly at an early age at the worst possible time for me as my father was terminally ill in hospital and my invalid mother and I were at his bedside in Southampton. The cats were in the care of two friends, and unfortunately it fell to one of them to break the news of her death to me. I often wonder whether I had been too distracted to notice that Topsy was ill or whether she had died suddenly of something that I could not have known about even had I been at home. Now I shall never know, as she had been buried by the time I came back home.

Sixteen years on Twinkle is still sharing my life, and she is even more accident prone now as her legs have become arthritic and her eyesight is not as good as it was. Despite all this she still tries optimistically to complete awkward jumps. She still fails and she still loves coffee.

What Difference does One More Make?

Topsy and Twinkle were about seven months old when my friend's mother, who had been ill for many years with cancer, was beginning to lose the battle that she had kept up for over twenty years. She was admitted into hospital and the news was rather bleak. Her daughter (another Pat) visited on a daily basis and then had to go to her mother's home to make sure the cat was okay. It was all very stressful and one day Pat said, 'I don't know what to do about the cat!'

At last I felt that I could be useful. 'Don't worry about the cat! That is the least of your problems. I've got three – what difference does one more make?'

Sadly her mother soon passed away and I offered to meet Pat at the house to help her sort through her belongings.

'You'd better bring the basket with you,' she said.

'Basket? What basket?' I asked, puzzled.

'The cat basket,' was the response, and I suddenly remembered my offer to have the cat, which I don't really think I believed I would ever be taken up on because her mother was such a fighter. That was how Tiddles became number four in my feline family.

I have to say that I don't think Tiddles was all that keen on her new living arrangements. She was a stocky, fat, white-and-tabby cat who had done nothing much with her life but laze around in the garden. She was none too keen on the idea of sharing a home with anyone, let alone three other cats, two still barely out of kittenhood, and she quickly cuffed everyone's ears to show her seniority and to ensure the respect that she felt went with it.

She was too scared to go down the flight of stairs to the garden, so she exchanged her outside life for one indoors, preferring to take fresh air on the ornamental balcony at the end of the lounge if the weather permitted.

For some reason she absolutely adored men, so Ted was welcomed to the house by this very rotund little cat. She would sit next to him or better still on him, all the while purring so much that she would dribble all over him. Fortunately he was a cat lover, and as none of the other three showed much interest in him, he and Tiddles became the greatest of friends and she looked forward to his visits.

Tiddles was about ten when she came to live with me, and a few years on she developed diabetes and needed daily insulin injections. She was actually quite good at being treated – it was usually me who messed up the administering of the insulin, and on several occasions I would ring the out-of-hours vet in a panic for advice over the telephone. When I had to go away for a few days to attend to family problems I had to find someone who was not squeamish to come over and administer her daily injection, and Tiddles behaved impeccably in the hands of a stranger I was told.

We kept her alive and reasonably healthy for nearly a year and then she went downhill rapidly – just at Christmas. Pat was spending the holidays with me and I gently warned her that she might not see her mother's cat again, although she could see for herself that the cat was unwell. Why do all my medical emergencies happen at holiday time? I had to ring the vet on New Year's Day – it was a young locum vet who was covering the surgery. He scratched his chin and checked her insulin dosage and suggested that we could try upping it until the next day when the regular vets would be back. I could see he was reticent about making any decision – and I do understand the reason why, but this was my cat and I knew that she had really had enough of being jabbed and having blood and urine tests taken, so I insisted that the decision was mine to make and Tiddles went to wait for me at Rainbow Bridge.

Chapter Three

Thomas Sets his Heart on Moving House

ONE OF THE CATS FED AND WATERED BY AN ELDERLY gentleman who lived up the road from me was an old black tomcat who had thus far evaded capture and therefore remained un-neutered. He was a notable cat with cauliflower ears, a pungent smell, and lumps and bumps all over him, each one the reminder of an old and untreated abscess acquired in fights with any rival male who happened to stray unwittingly into his territory.

Soon after my arrival in the area with my beautiful Tabatha, this old cat (who was eventually christened Thomas) decided that he wanted to move house and come and live with us. He started what I can only describe as a campaign that lasted several years to achieve those ends.

Tabatha had been spayed but this did not deter Thomas from his vigil outside the front door every spring in the hopes that she would venture out. I would open the front door to let Tabatha out and she would sniff the air from the safety of the doorstep. One whiff of his smell and that was it, she would rush back indoors and confine herself for several weeks until he got bored with waiting or until his male urges dissipated.

I always knew when Thomas had been in the house – he was never invited in, but if I left the open door unattended for a few seconds he would appear from nowhere and slink in behind me – as he always left his calling card: the awful smell of tomcat urine sprayed over doorstep, walls and anything else he could get his bottom near. That one cat could produce so much urine in so short a space of time never ceased to amaze me.

He was well known in the area, so I knew he had an owner of sorts and that at least he was fed and watered and given shelter whenever he needed it, but he remained determined to move house at the first possible opportunity, and he continued his campaign regardless of being shooed away by me.

My own cat family had now increased to four, and poor old Thomas must have wondered why all these cats were allowed to live with me when he was still denied access, or was it the fact that he fancied himself top cat in a house full of females that made him so determined?

I was looking out of my window one day in early summer when I noticed Thomas walking across the road. He was limping badly, hardly able to put one of his front paws on the ground. Try as I might I couldn't ignore him and went downstairs to have a closer look. There was certainly a problem with his paw and also, on closer examination, I could see that the top of his head was red-raw. As I looked him over, one of my neighbours came by and we both examined the poor old cat. Had he been hit by a car? I walked up the road with my neighbour as I helped her carry her heavy shopping, and Thomas followed painfully, determined not to let me get away now that I was showing some interest in him. As we stopped at her gate a few doors up, Thomas sat very close to me and again our attention fell on him.

'He's keeping very close to you,' my neighbour said. 'What are you going to do about him?'

I resolved that I would have to do something, even if he wasn't really my responsibility. I searched for the contact number of the local branch of the Cats Protection League that I had rung once before and explained the problem I had – or rather, the problems that Thomas was suffering. The re-assuring voice at the other end of the telephone said, 'Of course we will help. If we arrange for him to go to the vet would you be able to take him? We would pay all the costs, but would you be able to look after him until such time as we have a space to take him in?'

I would have said yes to anything at this point, so arrangements were made and Thomas was bundled into a basket and taken to the vet. I rang the next day to see how he was doing. He had been neutered and a large abscess in his paw had been drained and treated. The red-raw skin on his head was the result of frantic scratching to try and ease the discomfort in his ears caused by ear-mites, so there were eardrops to be administered for the next couple of weeks. What none of us could have known without the expertise of the vet was that Thomas had, at some point in time, been used for target practice by the nasty owner of an airgun as pellets were found in his side and rear quarters. The vet thought they had been there for some time, but decided they were better out than in. Just a day or so later Thomas came home a new man (and much less smelly), albeit minus a considerable patch of fur where the pellets had been removed.

I rang the kind lady from the Cats Protection League to let her know how he was doing and to thank her for her help. As we were talking I could see Thomas washing himself all over as he lazed in an armchair. He was actually beginning to look quite handsome in a rugged sort of way.

'Of course,' said the voice, 'it is very difficult to re-home cats of his age, and at the moment we don't have anywhere free to take him in. Would you be able to continue looking after him if we pay for veterinary treatment and food?'

Out of the corner of my eye I could see Thomas pause in his grooming activities. The silence hung in the air for a few seconds and than I found myself saying, 'Well, I suppose he is used to me and to the area around here. I can

27

cope with feeding him, but I would be very grateful for help with any vet bills.'

Thomas smiled – I'm sure he did! The deal was done and his campaign had finally reached a very satisfactory conclusion. He continued washing his fur nonchalantly, trying very hard to suppress the smirk on his face, and I became a volunteer for the Cats Protection League!

When Thomas officially joined the household after many years of trying to gain access we both tried very hard to make it work. I had grown to love him, but there was one major stumbling block which caused constant arguments and that was his inability to resist marking every inch of the house with urine. A family meeting was held between me, Thomas and all the other cats, who sniffed disdainfully at the affected areas on stairs and walls. Despite loud protestations from Thomas it was decided that he would have to move outside – especially now the weather was warm – and the porch was chosen to be his new home. A large cardboard box was found and filled with soft, warm bedding and a litter tray was provided for use on wet days or at night and food was provided at least twice a day. Thomas appeared to adapt quite easily to his new home and lifestyle, and he was allowed occasional forays indoors, although he seemed to know that each visit was just that: a visit.

Everything went well until the first winter when Thomas began to look more and more miserable. One of my rescue worker colleagues came up with the idea of building Thomas his own house. The intention was that his house would sit in my porch, so measurements were taken and a week or so later Thomas's new house arrived.

It was spectacular! Wall-to-wall carpeting throughout, a roof that lifted up for easy cleaning, two rooms and a window in the bedroom so that he could look out. An electrically heated pad was provided for those cold winter nights, and the outside had been varnished to give it extra protection. It sparkled in the wintry sunshine. Thomas loved his house and it was *his* house; none of the other cats showed any interest in it.

Visitors to my house would stand in the porch and admire Thomas's new home, and he never missed an opportunity to give anyone a quick tour of his property when they showed an interest: 'This is the door I go in… Look there is carpet for me to sharpen my claws on… Here is my bedroom – look I've got a window too.'

The specially designed and built cathouse provided warmth, shelter and comfort for Thomas over quite a number of years until he finally made the trip to Cat Heaven. The house was eventually moved to one of the sanctuaries where I like to think that some other poor old black cat was able to enjoy its amenities.

Mr Penfold was the elderly gentleman who had looked after Thomas until he managed to move in with me. He was obviously impressed by my ability to pick Thomas up and give him a cuddle.

'To be honest, mate, he used to scare me a bit,' he would say of Thomas.

Mr Penfold was around eighty years old and was always to be seen dressed in scruffy clothes with a little woolly hat on his head. He appeared to have two of these: the winter one had a pompom on the top whilst the summer one didn't. He had an assortment of cats, all of which he had taken in as strays and all of whom were called 'Mate' – except that is, for 'Baby'. All the humans in Mr Penfold's life were also called 'Mate', which made conversations quite confusing.

The cats had all been neutered by the Cats Protection League long before my time, but once I had arrived on the scene Mr Penfold became one of my ongoing case problems, not that I minded, as he was quite a sweet old boy. I would often see him struggling up the road with a bag full of shopping and I knew that there were bound to be several tins of cat food and a couple of chickens for the cats. He would de-bone the chickens once they were cooked and then chop them up before he gave them to the cats, but there any finesse stopped abruptly, as the roughly diced chicken would then be spread quite literally on one end of the kitchen table whilst he sat and ate his dinner at the other end.

Occasionally, armed with a tin of flea spray, a couple of us would go up to Mr Penfold's flat, where we would be met at the door by Mr Penfold in his long johns – his clothes, such as they were, appeared to be reserved for outdoor pursuits like shopping. Cats, flat and (if the truth be known) even Mr Penfold himself would be sprayed liberally. We even gave his bed a quick squirt as we knew the cats slept with him.

I was always aware when Mr Penfold had a problem with one of his cats as I would see him standing on the other side of the road looking up at the house in the hope that I would come out into the garden. He never came to knock at the door, which would have been much easier, and when I could ignore him no longer I would go out to see him.

'Hello, Mr Penfold. Have you got a problem with one of your cats?' I would ask.

'Yes, Mate,' he'd reply.

'Which one?' I'd ask optimistically.

'Mate,' he'd answer helpfully!

I took many of Mr Penfold's cats to the vet over the years. Our jovial vet, who knew of Mr Penfold but didn't have any personal knowledge of the gentleman, would look at me with a twinkle in his eye and ask, 'Now which cat is this? Mate?'

On one occasion to my horror this regular repartee was followed by, 'I hope you haven't been cuddling this one – it's got *lice*!'

Gradually the number of cats dwindled through natural causes and Mr Penfold would ask me to take a very sick cat to the vet.

'Bring him home, Mate,' he would say, 'so I can bury him in the garden.'

Thankfully they had all gone to Cat Heaven by the time Mr Penfold had to go into a residential care home where, I heard from neighbours, he was having the time of his life and now had a lady friend to occupy his time!

Thomas was very old. When he had first gone to the vet his age was estimated to be above ten, and by talking to neighbours and Mr Penfold I discovered that he was probably well over that and was more likely to have been between eighteen and twenty by the time he was put to sleep. Everyone in the road knew him – he had those notable cauliflower ears and he was always sitting in the front garden, so you couldn't miss him as you walked by the house. I knew he had a slight thyroid problem, but it didn't seem to affect him much and the vet thought it was better left alone if it gave him no problems rather than to risk operating on this elderly cat. Thomas carried on quite happily for another four or five years and then he suddenly began to look as though life was a struggle. I came home from work one day and saw him sitting in the garden – he looked miserable. I rang the vet and got an immediate appointment. Laura was to examine him as she did all my animals at that time, and as I entered her consulting room I found myself saying, 'I'm not really expecting to take this cat home.'

She knew that I did not believe in prolonging the life of my animals unnecessarily; in my opinion (and I am well aware that there are others out there who do not share my views) it is the last kind deed I can do for the pets I have loved and shared my life with to make that last, hard decision and end their suffering.

'I think he has probably only got about another month to go,' she said after examining him, 'and if you have made your decision today, I think we should go ahead and put him to sleep.'

This was the end of an era, the end of his campaign to gain my love – a love which I gave very readily when he joined my family officially, and I am sure that when my time comes his poor, beaten-up old face with its cauliflower ears will be one of the first that comes to greet me at Rainbow Bridge.

Chapter Four

The Telephone Starts to Ring

WHEN THOMAS FINALLY CAME TO THE END OF HIS life I had been working for the Cats Protection League for several years. After their initial help with his veterinary costs, I decided to write a letter of thanks to the local branch of the Cats Protection League who had been so instrumental in helping this poor old cat. I offered my services if there was anything I could do to help them in their work – little did I know how this simple little letter of thanks would change my life forever!

In the beginning I started as I suppose most people do by fostering a cat or two and helping at jumble sales and bazaars, but soon I found my telephone number was being advertised for members of the public to ring to receive financial help towards the neutering of their cats.

'I want my cat done,' was a favourite, followed by, 'I want my cat nurtured… spayded… muted,' and even one memorable individual who said, 'I don't know what it's called, but I want it done to my cat!'

I found myself picking up cats and delivering them to the vet for the operation and then taking them back to their owners afterwards as no one appeared to have a car, a cat basket or to even have heard of public transport, and of course they always had the kids to pick up, which meant that they could never take their own cats to the vet at the appointed time.

I had taken a male cat to be castrated and delivered him safely back home. When I came home from work the next day, there was a message on my answering machine from the owner asking me to ring, urgently! I rang immediately and the owner's voice was quite hysterical.

'My cats' balls have exploded!' he said.

I promised to be there within half an hour, and en route I wondered what awful scene would greet me – I imagined fur and blood on ceiling and walls, and wished that I were a little less squeamish about the sight of blood!

On my arrival I was relieved to find that the cat seemed to be less perturbed by his wounds than the owner, and although a small opening had appeared on his rear end, it didn't appear to worry him. However, I whipped him off to the vet yet again where they put a bit of antiseptic powder on the wound and assured me that it was all perfectly normal and would heal in a couple of days.

My telephone soon became red hot with a flood of calls requesting all manner of feline help: calls about un-neutered tomcats breaking in through cat flaps, beating up on resident cats and eating their food then spraying everywhere by way of thanks.

Advice on how to stop cats spraying was a great favourite and I knew all the theories – my own cats, unfortunately, refused to adhere to any of them. One very nice and very concerned owner rang me one day to say that she had a cat and a dog and they had lived together in harmony for years, but suddenly her cat had taken to spraying all over the dog's bed – she never did it anywhere else. As we chatted I learned that she had recently had her kitchen refitted and because the dog's bed was bigger they had swapped the position of his bed with the cat's bed that had a bigger space by the radiator. I laughed as I said, 'Well, if I was your cat and you had moved my bed from its nice warm spot by the radiator, I think I'd spray on your dog's bed too!'

'Do you really think it could just be that?' she asked incredulously. I didn't hear from her again, so I guess she must have switched the beds back and resolved her problems.

One lady called with a big problem: a mother cat had decided to have her four kittens in a shed in her garden. She bred Labradors and couldn't bring the cat and kittens indoors, but was terribly worried that foxes might get the kittens when they started to move around.

Arrangements to collect the cat and kittens were underway when the lady rang me again. Someone had been to see the kittens and wanted one of them, but she didn't like the man in question as she thought he might be a breeder who had something wrong with his breeding stock and wanted to introduce new blood as he was only interested in the one male kitten. I told her not to worry as the kittens were coming to us so he would have to go through a home-check before we released anything to him, and we would surely be able to sound him out at that time. I told her to give him my telephone number if he came back to her. Eventually he did ring and left a message on my answering machine; I rang him back and when I asked for him by name, a very cultured voice said, 'And which one do you want? There are two people by that name in this house.'

I explained who I was and which person I wanted to speak to. When I finally spoke to the right person he said that I had got his kitten and he wanted it immediately. I kept calm and replied that I was not aware of any written agreement that made the kitten his property and that in fact all four kittens and their mother had been legally signed over to the CPL for re-homing and this was what had happened; all four kittens and their mother had gone to new homes. Realising that I would not be budged, he said in a very superior voice, 'Madam, may I just say one thing?'

'Of course,' I replied.

'B*****ks to it!' he said and slammed the receiver down!

One Christmas Day morning I received a call about a cat that had been lying in a garden for four days. Christmas Eve had been a particularly frosty night and the people thought they'd better do something in case the cat died. Why they hadn't decided to do anything on the three days leading up to Christmas Day I will never understand. Anyway, the turkey was put on hold and arrangements were made to get the cat picked up and taken to our vet where they are on call twenty-four hours a day, every day of the year.

The poor cat was only about a year old. She had a broken pelvis and had also had to fight as hard as she could to protect herself from foxes as she lay in pain in that garden for four days. Once recovered from her injuries she was found a loving home where I am sure her new owners still relate the traumas that the little cat had to endure. Hopefully she will only ever have a happy Christmas from now onwards.

On another occasion I was called to collect a cat that had been involved in a road traffic accident, and as I gently lifted the injured cat into a basket the stench hit me and followed me in the car all the way to the vet. The full scale of the cat's injuries soon became apparent, and the wound was full of maggots, no doubt due to the very hot summer weather.

'No matter how many years you spend doing cat work,' the vet said, 'you will probably never see another case as bad as this one.'

The maggots had spread a long way inside the poor little cat's body and the only option was to end its misery, so I stood stroking the limp little body while the vet administered the drug and the cat gently slipped away into a never-ending sleep.

Another lady was moving house and she didn't want her cat anymore, please would I come and take it away now! I explained that we were full and did not have any spaces to take her cat into at this moment.

'What do you mean no spaces?' she snapped back at me.

I went on to explain that we were not a sanctuary and we fostered in our own homes for the most part and that there was therefore a limit to the number of cats that we were able to take in. She did not understand this and replied angrily, 'You're the CPL, what does it matter how many cats you have?'

Unfortunately, we can't wave a magic wand and resolve every cat problem that comes along – we do try very hard though, and I often wonder what happens to the ones we can't help.

'I've found a kitten under a pile of wood in my garden,' said a voice on the telephone one day.

I rushed off with a basket to see this kitten hoping that it was not a 'kitten' of more than ten years old and on its last legs as was more usually the case, but this time it *was* a kitten of about five weeks old. We searched the garden for more and then asked neighbours but no one knew anything about it. How did a friendly little kitten of such a young age appear under a pile of wood on its own? I never did find out, and the kitten was homed once it had recovered from its ordeal.

There was also a stream of calls from people wanting their cats re-homed for various reasons, ranging from the arrival of a new baby or grandchild, asthma in the family, emigration, moving from a house to a flat, marriage break-ups or one quite memorable caller who wanted to get rid of the cat because they had new furniture arriving and they did not want the cat using the new settee as a scratching post! There were also the calls where elderly owners had died thus rendering their poor cats homeless. Sometimes it was possible to resolve difficulties over the telephone by talking through the problems being experienced and giving advice to try and ensure that their cat did not have to be uprooted, but sometimes there were more callous owners who really had quite simply tired of having a cat around.

One evening I answered a knock at my front door and found a man standing there with a tiny tabby kitten in his hands.

'I've found a kitten in my garden,' he said.

He lived in my road, and knowing most of the cat owners in the neighbourhood, I dispensed with all the normal questions, suspecting that his children had come home with the kitten, which had probably been handed out after school by one of their friends only to be met by a less than impressed mother and father. I took the kitten in and resolved not to give it a name, thus ensuring that the kitten was re-homed. Any cat or kitten who had a name chosen by me often seemed to stay forever.

Within days another kitten came to stay and the pair became inseparable, one tabby and the other black with a white tummy. Enter Martin, a colleague at work.

Martin wanted a kitten for his two sons and preferably he wanted a tabby. I asked him if he would consider taking a pair but he was adamant he only wanted the one kitten. Enter his two female work-mates: they decided he was going to have both my kittens and they began their campaign to weaken his resolve. I admit that I did play a supporting role. Poor Martin opened his lunchbox one day and found a poster inside with the following notice written on it in black marker pen:

'My step-brother has found a new Dad, but his new Dad doesn't want me!'

Underneath was the picture of a little black cat!

Martin went to get in his car to go home and found another notice under his windscreen wipers:

'My step-brother's new Dad doesn't want me because I'm black!'

For several days Martin couldn't open a file without a poster flying out. There was a poster on the door to his office, on the wall behind his desk and – I'm told – there was even a poster in the gents' toilet! One morning, as I sat at my desk with the first coffee of the day in my hands, Martin poked his head around my office door as he went past.

'I'll have them both!' he said, and then he carried on along the corridor to his own office.

I rushed after him and protested that he didn't really have to take them both; I did understand that he only wanted one, but he had made up his mind!

His two lovely sons knew nothing of the surprise he had arranged for them, and they were over the moon when I arrived at their house one Friday evening with two kittens in a basket. They immediately got down on the floor and played with the kittens and started to select possible names for their new pets. Suddenly Danny, the younger of the two and the true cat lover in the family, said, 'Dad, Mum does know about this, doesn't she?' His joy at getting the two kittens was suddenly clouded by the possible reaction of his mother – he could see that if Mum didn't know, the kittens' stay in his home might be cut short.

Martin (a renowned practical joker) reassured him that Mum did know, and they cautiously went back to playing with the kittens and choosing names. Then Mum came home. Her eyes fell on the scene in her kitchen and her face looked like thunder! I heard her whisper to Martin, 'I said *one* kitten!'

I made my excuses and beat a hasty retreat!

The kittens are now cats and still live with Martin and his family, and even Mum has fallen under their spell!

Chapter Five

Ziggy, the Sweet-Toothed Leader of the Pack

IN THE EIGHTEEN MONTHS OF HIS LIFE BEFORE COMING to live with me – initially as a foster cat – Ziggy had already had five homes to our certain knowledge. The last of these was a family with five children who were all on the 'At Risk' register. This perhaps explained why he was so petrified and spent the first few days in the ceiling space of my utility room – a feat never even contemplated by the many previous foster cats lodging in the room.

Ziggy was a muscular black-and-white cat with a black tail, the tip of which was white – just as though it had been dipped into a pot of white paint – with big round eyes that grew more saucer-like as he encountered situations that scared him. His fur was matted, but after investigation by the vet it was established that he had been daubed with glue – perhaps from the sticky hands of the children who had shared his last home.

Ziggy gradually became bolder and started to mix with the other cats, and he quickly became the cat that most of the others respected. He was never aggressive to them, but he was considered the leader of the pack – and I think this surprised even him at times!

At about the same time I had a lovely tabby called Zoe staying with me, and Ziggy really did like her. They were playing in the garden one day as I was hanging out the washing. I watched them romping around and then Zoe went indoors for a snoop inside the utility room. The pond in the garden was surrounded by patio on one side and a bed of heathers on the other. Ziggy cowered beneath the heathers waiting for Zoe to come back onto the patio, and as I watched her coming down the steps from the back door, I suddenly realised what Ziggy had in mind.

'Be careful, Ziggy!' I called out too late. He leapt from his hiding position across to the patio – at least, that was what he meant to do, but instead he landed with a splash in the middle of the very muddy pond. Zoe looked at him with total disdain as he hauled himself out of the pond, and forgetting the object of his previous desires, he walked over to me, shivering with the shock and coldness of the water. He looked a state; even his white fur was now a muddy grey. I scooped him up and took him indoors to dry him off.

Zoe was eventually found a new home and her new owners only wanted one cat, but when they saw Ziggy I could see them wavering and thinking that maybe they could cope with two. I found myself saying, 'Sorry, I'm keeping this one,' and this was how Ziggy became the first of my foster cats to be officially adopted.

Ziggy was quite a brave cat, never one to turn away from a fight, but he went into these forays knowing that he was never going to win. He spent more than enough time in the veterinary surgery after each fight because he always developed an abscess requiring a course of antibiotics.

'You should tie a white flag to his tail before he goes outside,' said the vet one day after treating Ziggy for yet another abscess.

Kittens loved Ziggy for some reason, and he seemed to take quite well to them. He would play so roughly with them that in the beginning I was worried he might injure them he was so strong. I would watch him throw them up in the air and then sit on them, then he would have a mad five minutes rushing around the room followed by three or four kittens before landing on one of them, pinning it to the ground. The kitten would squirm and wriggle, but Ziggy would sit tight and look nonchalantly around the room, then, just as suddenly, he would jump off and run away. The kitten would hide under a chair and wait for Ziggy to come back, which he always did, and then I would see the kitten's bottom begin to wriggle, preparing to jump out on Ziggy to scare him as he went passed. Ziggy never failed to feign surprise. Then they'd all go racing off around the room again and the whole process would repeat itself.

The new cat next door was also black-and-white, but barely out of kittenhood when I first saw him. Ziggy had just gone out of the front door, and as I watched him walking slowly down the side of the house, his tail in the air, the kitten from next door jumped up on the wall and followed him, tail also erect, and both cats had the very same white tip at the top of their tail. My neighbour, who was also watching, shared the humour of the scene – Ziggy and Son of Ziggy; a real case of following in father's footsteps, although Ziggy wasn't his real father, of course.

At one time a new rescue cat brought cat flu into the house and Ziggy and Oliver suffered more than any of the other cats. Both were admitted into veterinary hospital for intensive treatment. After four days it was thought that they might respond more quickly at home, and I am sure that had he not come home that very day, Ziggy would have given up and died. When I got him out of the basket his obvious pleasure at being back home with me again brought tears to my eyes. I still had to force-feed him, but he accepted it, and within days the change in him was remarkable.

At night, Ziggy would sleep on my shoulder and I would fall asleep listening to his low rumbling purr in my ear. He was the only one of my cats who became the owner rather than the owned; Ziggy owned me, and he made it very clear to cats and humans alike that he had all rights over me. He would sit between me and anyone else on the settee, and he would oust any cat who dared to sit on my knee. I very often found myself with three or four cats hanging on for dear life to the little spot on my quite ample knee that he occasionally allowed them to share. My knees resembled a pincushion, covered in tiny pinprick marks from the claws that had dug into my flesh to stop their owners falling off! When family circumstances meant that I had to leave the cats in the care of friends for a few days, Ziggy left home too and took up residence in the greenhouse, much to the consternation of the carers. He came home the moment he heard my voice, bounding up the garden and in through the window!

Ziggy was very particular about where he had his meals. He would wait patiently by his place mat while bowls were put out for the other cats to rush to and then, last of all, his plate was put in front of him. He liked this particular place to eat because it was next to the biscuit bowl and he would lift a piece of cat food from his bowl and place it in the biscuit bowl then eat it. Sometimes I would remember that he liked biscuits with his food and put a few on top of his bowl saving him this ritual. He also had a sweet tooth and liked cake; on the odd occasion he was given some he would drop it on the floor and put his paw over it, growling at any cat that passed by before scoffing it down quickly. Custard, tinned creamed rice pudding, ice cream and ordinary cream were all favourites and came in useful when he was ill and needed something to disguise the taste of pills. I often wondered whether he had developed a sweet tooth after being fed cake by the children in the families he had lived with before coming to stay with me.

I was going to make some cakes for a bazaar one day, and wanting something quick and easy I visited the local Weigh and Save shop for some bags of cake mix – one plain and one ginger. I had some stemmed ginger at home left over from Christmas, and my mouth watered at the thought of the ginger cake I was going to make later that day.

I unpacked my shopping in the kitchen and absentmindedly placed the bags of cake mix on the work surface, intending to start baking later that day. However, I became distracted as often happens and the cake mixture stayed on the work surface for the remainder of the afternoon. Suddenly I heard a thud in the kitchen, followed by a lot of rustling. Whatever were those cats doing now? I went out to investigate and there, in the middle of the floor, sat Ziggy surrounded by what remained of the two plastic bags filled with cake mix. The bags had been ripped open and the contents were now strewn all over the floor. Some of the cake mix bore the signs of having been well licked, and Ziggy had cake mix all over his face and paws. He looked at me with an expression on his face that seemed to say, 'I don't know how it happened, but it wasn't me, Mum, honestly!'

Sadly, after eleven years of companionship and love I was shocked to learn that Ziggy had developed an aggressive tumour on his liver and he survived for only a short time after diagnosis. The strength of my grief surprised me and concerned my poor vet, who was seriously worried that I might not make the short journey home due to the state I was in. He led me off into the staff kitchen to have a cup of tea before ushering me, still sobbing, out of the back door. I framed a photograph of Ziggy and hung it on my lounge wall, and I often find myself talking to it as I pass by. I still miss him today, but I draw comfort from the belief that we will be reunited one day at Rainbow Bridge.

Chapter Six

Posey, a Purrfect Little Cat…

OF ALL THE CATS THAT HAVE SHARED MY LIFE OR WILL do in the future, none could compare with Posey. I remember the day I found out about her as clearly as though it was yesterday: 'There is a cat at the vet's, a dear little tabby with big blue eyes – I wondered if you would collect her and foster her?'

That was the telephone call that changed my life and gave me a loyal and constant friend and companion for the next dozen or so years. The vet had obviously fallen under her spell too. 'She is the dearest little cat,' he said when I went to collect her. 'We thought initially that she was only a kitten, but when I looked at her closely I decided that she is at least six months old, so I have spayed her, but she is so badly under-nourished that she hasn't really grown much. She has got chlamydia so she needs antibiotics and eye ointment, and I'd like to see her again in a couple of weeks' time.'

Once home, I took her out of the basket and I knew deep in my heart that she would be staying. She had come from a notorious multi-cat household where the Cats Protection League were gradually trying to get all the cats neutered and either returned or re-homed – a task that went on for several years before drawing to a satisfactory conclusion with all the cats having been neutered.

She was indeed the most beautiful little tabby, with slate-blue eyes, and I had known her name before she arrived as I had already decided that the next female cat that came into my care would be called Posey. This name suited her most admirably; it was obviously meant to be!

Posey was, quite simply, adorable. She had a zest for life and a love for humans and cats alike. Those initial days were quite frightening as she was hyperactive and had breathing difficulties because of her blocked-up nose, and sometimes she would be gasping for breath as she chased around the room. She would quite literally sleep where she fell because she would keep going until her eyelids couldn't stay open any longer – I often found myself offering her some spent matchsticks so she could try to keep her eyes open a little longer. She ate anything and everything, seemingly trying to make up for the deprivation of her early months. Most of all, she wanted to be cuddled and fussed and quickly became an extension of me as I carried her around with me as one would a baby, never ceasing to amaze myself by what I could achieve with a cat in one arm and a tin-opener in the other!

Two weeks later, we were back to see the vet.

'This isn't the little cat that we had in here, is it?' When I confirmed that it was the same cat, he continued, 'Goodness! Hasn't she grown? She likes her food, doesn't she? Haven't you done well with her?'

I bristled with pride. I admit: Posey's tummy was now noticeably rotund. Her eyes were still runny and so was her nose, so we went home with another course of antibiotics and eye ointment. These trips to see the vet continued on a regular basis for the next six months or so, and occasionally Posey was admitted to have the ulcers on her eyelids scraped. The last of these occasions gave me great cause for concern as Posey appeared to react badly to the anaesthetic. I resolved at that point that I didn't mind a cat with a rather snotty nose and runny eyes and took her off the homing list immediately.

As she grew older Posey's trips to see the vet became less

frequent; we only went for more antibiotics when the eyes began to look very sore and the nose became even more congested. I always wished that I could teach her to blow into a handkerchief, but she was never able to master that, despite all my efforts.

Did you ever have a comfort blanket as a child? Well, Posey did, although her 'blanket' was a long length of plastic string which she used to take everywhere with her. It was filthy dirty and had been knotted many times to stop it fraying, but she loved it. She would chatter away to it – heaven knows what she expected it to say back – and I would find this mucky piece of string all over the house, discarded only for a minute or two until she remembered where she had left it. She would sit with her front paws on the arm of my chair and pat my arm gently in the hopes that she could make my arm go down to the floor and pick up that string and play with it: it usually did! It also worked with everyone else that she tried – you just couldn't resist her big blue eyes staring into your face and the tap, tap, tap of her paw on your arm! On the rare occasions that you had the nerve to carry on watching television and ignore her, she would go over to the talking box and, standing on her back legs, commence pawing at the screen, occasionally stopping to look back over her shoulder to see whether you had picked up her string. If not, she continued pawing the screen until you relented!

Everyone knew and loved Posey. She was the only cat who really welcomed visitors to the house, and would want to sit on their knee or play with them – she'd even sneeze all over them if I dropped my guard for a moment – but nobody seemed to mind. The other cats would go to Posey when they felt in need of a cuddle, and Posey would never turn them away. She also had this endearing habit of chattering away to herself, and sometimes I would ask her what she was talking about. She would look at me with those big blue eyes as if to say, 'It's all right, I wasn't talking to anyone, I'm just playing.'

Posey loved any and every new experience in life, and so it was with Christmas. As Christmas Day approached so did the decorations: the walls and ceiling were festooned with streamers and balloons. The Christmas tree was assembled and decorated with all manner of baubles and chocolate novelties wrapped in silver paper, and a fairy sat at the top, wide-eyed and smiling into the room. Oh, how Posey loved Christmas – even before the day arrived. She loved the dangly things hanging from the ceiling and tried desperately to jump up and catch them, and she especially loved that Christmas tree.

On returning home the day before Christmas Eve I noticed a small silver ball near the front door in the hall. My suspicions aroused, I investigated further and found the beautiful Christmas tree had mysteriously toppled over, and then I noticed all the silver paper strewn over the carpet. Each of the chocolate shapes that had decorated my tree had been carefully unwrapped by sharp little claws, the chocolate discarded in favour of the sparkling wrapping paper.

For ten days Posey walked round the house looking towards the ceiling, her little mind trying to work out how best to get to the decorations which fluttered tantalisingly above her head. She jumped on the backs of the chairs, tried from the top of the sideboard and then just jumped from the floor to see how high she could get. Finally she tried the bureau: if she climbed onto the top of the bureau and stood on tip-toes on her back feet, she could just about get an extended paw onto the bottom of one of the streamers and pull it down. The wallpaper did not stand up to this type of treatment anymore than the streamers!

Sweets, or the paper they were wrapped in, provided Posey with yet another form of amusement: every time a sweet was unwrapped she demanded the paper. By the time Boxing Day was drawing to a close the floor was littered with screwed up balls of coloured paper – the remnants of

Posey's attempts to play football. And then we had some snow. None of the other cats would go out: Posey wouldn't come in! She adored the snow. She tried to catch the flakes in her paws, but she couldn't work out where they had gone as she was sure she had caught them. She didn't mind falling in a snowdrift or the fact that her paws were cold and her coat damp; this was a new experience and she was going to explore it until she had no questions left unanswered.

Finally, Christmas drew towards the end. An almighty crash heralded the final demise of the Christmas tree as Posey decided to depose the fairy at the top. Cats and humans flew in all directions; that was fun too! Posey cried as all those much adored decorations were taken down and put into boxes. She spent the evening looking towards the ceiling with occasional sad little meows as she mourned the loss of such a wonderful source of entertainment.

Through her own choice Posey didn't go outside very often, mostly because there was much more going on indoors and she didn't want to miss anything, but one of her favourite pastimes was to stand with her back feet on the inside window sill and her front paws hanging over the bottom of the open window. She would hang out of the window like this for ages, just watching the world go by.

Posey always seemed to know when I was upset and she always knew if I had a problem because I would talk it through with her first. She would stand as usual with her back feet on the floor and her front feet on the arm of my chair, then she would pat my arm before creeping up onto my knee, purring softly and looking at me as though she were saying, 'There, there, it will be all right, I'm here.'

Posey had cancer and I was devastated; the vet suggested that we try a course of chemotherapy on her as this had proved successful with other cats, but the cancer would not be abated and I finally had to accept that it was her time to leave me as she had finally lost her zest for life. She was put to sleep as she lay peacefully in my arms. Thus I lost the perfect friend that I had shared so much with for so many happy years. She will never be replaced: no other cat could have her eyes and such a perfect temperament. She never had a cross moment in her life, and I can still feel the silkiness of her fur and the comforting warmth of her body in my arms.

…And Daisy, a Loving Little Cat

Daisy was a black cat about eighteen months old when she came to me; a lovely, friendly little cat with a really cheeky nature. She came from the same source as Posey, and although she arrived only a few weeks later than the little blue-eyed tabby, I don't think they recognised each other. The amazing thing about both cats was that despite their awful start in life they had the most loveable temperaments – neither of them ever fought with the other cats or had a bad day.

Daisy and Posey quickly formed the official welcoming party for visitors to my house, which was rather nerve-racking for me as they both had runny noses so I had to keep the tissues close by, ready to rush into nose-cleaning action at the first sign of a sneeze! Everyone loved both cats as they would accommodate anyone daft enough to play with them or cuddle them. Posey did not like it when Daisy or any of the other cats played with her string, and she would sit watching the antics with a disapproving look on her face until the string was dangled in her direction, at which she would sit on the end and haul the string in with her sharp little claws until it was all piled up in a heap under her plump little body. Daisy was never bothered by these displays of disapproval, and simply looked for something else to play with.

Daisy was a menace for putting things in her mouth – especially anything plastic or pieces of string. The times I had to pull a long piece of soggy string or cotton from her mouth it's a wonder she didn't ever have to undergo an operation to remove something from her stomach!

Daisy merged into the household from the day she arrived, and although her health problems were similar to Posey's they were also less severe, but this didn't prevent me from frequently having to administer antibiotics and eye ointment to one very wriggly and uncooperative black cat. The health problems they both endured for their entire lives could have been prevented if their original owner had only had her cats neutered so that they could not interbreed. Daisy's tear ducts were almost non-existent, which left her with a permanent stream of tears running down her face, and Posey's were so small that they couldn't cope with the fluid and would eventually become blocked, which must have been painful. However, if the owner had not allowed her cat family to expand out of control I may never have experienced the pleasure of the company of these two little darlings! My only regret is that dear little Daisy spent her whole life trying to be more than second best to Posey, and although I loved her dearly I could never quite convince her that she was at least as good as Posey!

One Christmas I noticed that the fur on Daisy's head appeared all spiked up, and gradually I noticed a lump forming under it. I rushed her to the vet as soon as they opened after the holiday period and it emerged that she had a tumour inside her head. There was nothing they could do for her except to ensure that she was not in any pain, and over the next two months I watched the tumour grow down one side of her face. She was still eager for food and she was still purring, but she was not quite so eager to play. The tumour continued to grow until it finally became visible down her nostril, and at that point she had a good long cuddle and sadly made her final trip to see the vet.

Chapter Seven

Oliver, a Single-Minded Cat

MY FIRST EVER 'RESCUE' JOB FOR THE CATS PROTECTION League was to collect and then foster a cat that had been left behind by its owners when they moved house. Armed with a cat basket, loads of enthusiasm and very little else, this naïve volunteer set off on her mission to pick up this cat and rescue him from his situation of distress. The cat (who was later called Oliver) had his own ideas about the situation he was in, as I was soon to discover when the new occupiers of his house met me at the gate…

'There he is,' said the new male owner of the house, pointing towards a rather handsome, long-haired tabby with a white chest and paws, sitting placidly at the bottom of their garden. As I gently approached the cat, a loud male voice shouted, 'Be careful! He's a bit feisty!'

At this Oliver shot off across the garden and under the shed. He scowled at me from the darkness as I peered in to see whether I could make a grab at him. 'You'll not catch him now,' the man said, revelling in my show of inexperience in catching cats. 'He'll stay there until it gets dark now.'

I bowed to his greater knowledge and experience and said I would come back the next morning, asking them not to feed him until I arrived.

Fortunately for me Oliver loved his food, and so the next day, after lulling him into a false sense of security with a bowl of Whiskas, I made a grab and in one moment of sheer luck on my part he was bundled into the awaiting basket. He was truly a handsome cat, with saucer-like eyes of yellowish-green, long white whiskers and a very pink nose. His fur was a mass of knots after having lived rough for a month or two, but I felt sure it was nothing I couldn't sort out with regular grooming. Oliver had his own ideas about that too, and just the sight of me with the brush in my hand would turn this beautiful cat into a thing demented!

My mother and father had recently lost their tabby cat, Charlie, to a road accident. Charlie had just turned up on their doorstep one day, and having the same animal-orientated genes as me they had taken him into their home and their hearts and they were devastated by his loss – especially as it came in such a violent manner. Dad had set his heart on another tabby, so Oliver packed his bags and made the long journey from London to Southampton to start a new life, where my mother, having time and patience to spare, managed to sort out Oliver's fur and return it to its former glory – although he still would not allow her to comb his tummy.

All's well that ends well, I thought, until three weeks later when I received a telephone call from my mother who was in tears.

'We've lost Oliver,' she sniffed down the telephone. 'He went out this morning for the first time and the dog next door barked at him and frightened him off.' More sobs filled my ears.

'Don't worry,' I said, 'he'll come home when he gets hungry.'

'But he doesn't know where he lives,' she retorted, still sobbing and sniffing at me.

'Of course he does,' I continued, hoping that I sounded more confident than I felt. 'He's spent three weeks looking out of the window, Mum, so he knows which garden is his – he's not silly.'

She remained unconvinced I could tell, but she made her excuses and rang off to go and try calling him again.

An hour or so later, the telephone rang again. 'He's come home!' said an excited voice at the other end of the line. 'He just came in through the patio doors and cried for his dinner, so I gave him some fish that I had cooked especially.'

Oliver lived quite happily with my parents for the next five years, and during that time they revelled in the compliments they received from friends and neighbours alike about their handsome cat. Sadly, ill health meant that eventually Mum and Dad had to exchange their home for residential care and Oliver had to pack his bags once more and retrace his steps, this time from Southampton to London where he lived with me and the other cats.

Oliver did not like a great deal of attention, and when he grew tired of being stroked and petted he would let you know it and scratch or bite your hand quite fiercely. He didn't like the other cats much either, so he kept himself to himself for the most part. He was an avid hunter and would leave his half-eaten prey all over the lawn – even after he had to have all his teeth removed, which resulted in the tendency to sit with his tongue hanging out!

He was a nightmare when it came to administering pills as well, and I would have to wrap him tightly in a towel to save myself from any permanent damage. When he and Ziggy caught cat flu from one of the rescue cats I had taken in I was relieved when the vet took over and admitted them into hospital. They both came out in four or five days and while Ziggy improved, Oliver did not and had to return to see the senior vet who admitted him again. The vet had to force feed him, and when he had recovered enough to be sent home I went to collect him and speak to the vet.

'What a good cat he is,' said the vet. 'When I was drip-feeding him he just lay in my arms and took the tube down his throat – he was no trouble at all.'

Had the vet become confused – was this really *my* Oliver he was talking about? I was surprised he still had any hands left! He lifted Oliver out of the basket and put him on the table, and as if someone had pushed a button Oliver rolled over on the table, purring loudly and butting the vet's hand with his head, waiting for a stroke. I couldn't believe it. Every time he had to go to the vet after that we saw the same vet, and Oliver never forgot him and he would go through the same display of love time and time again.

Oliver lived for another eight years, but towards the end of his life he developed quite a few health issues and I seemed to be continually popping pills down his throat. Thankfully he accepted this more readily than he had done in the past – he had mellowed considerably. He now sat on my knee, purring all the time, and I very rarely received an injury from his sharp claws. He did occasionally take my hand in his mouth as if he were biting, but all I felt was a very soggy, hot, gummy jaw now that his teeth had gone.

He finally went to join the other cats in Heaven and to be reunited with my parents who, no doubt, are sitting on their cloud to this day, proudly showing him off to all the angels!

Chapter Eight

Pixie-Devil, a Cat with Attitude

I WAS ASKED TO FOSTER A CAT THAT WAS NO LONGER wanted by her owners, but before arrangements for her collection were finalised she was taken away at the owner's request by the Animal Wardens attached to the local council. Someone was sent to try and retrieve her and I awaited her arrival that evening.

'I don't know what you are going to do with this one,' said my colleague as she brought the cat basket in through the door. 'She's a real horror, we had ever such a problem getting her into the basket.'

Once inside the security of the utility room, I tentatively opened the basket and out came the most beautiful white cat – white, that is, with the exception of her tail which was tortoiseshell from top to bottom, and a few flashes of colour on the top of her head. She hissed, spat and howled all at the same time it seemed, and with nostrils flaring and ears laid back, Pixie announced her arrival to join my cat family. Her name was chosen by my mother, and was a choice based upon my description of this ferocious animal.

That evening I fed her and talked to her, but she made it quite clear that if I dared to touch her she would make mincemeat of me, so I left her to settle for the night. The next morning her attitude had not mellowed at all. I dared to attempt a stroke and immediately teeth and claws mauled my arm.

'Whatever has happened to your arm?' asked my work colleagues later that day.

'Oh, it was just a traumatised and unhappy cat that I took in last night,' I replied, hoping that I sounded unconcerned and nonchalant about my injuries that actually hurt like hell!

Pixie's tale of woe gradually unfolded; her owner had bought her as a kitten and kept her for some eighteen months, during which time she had scratched the furniture to shreds. In an attempt to stop her causing such damage her owner had smacked her every time she was 'naughty'. Pixie, therefore, had grown up to believe that hands were only there to administer punishment, and she had quickly learned to defend herself in the only way she could; attack before being attacked yourself. So I knew what her problem was, but how to overcome her insecurities was another matter...

Someone suggested that I use a gauntlet to save my hand from further injury, but this only sent Pixie into a display of even greater ferocity – she obviously thought this gloved hand could do her even more harm. I decided that the only way to deal with her was to put my hand near her and let her do whatever she wanted to it. I had to teach her that hands were not just there to administer punishment; they could also do nice things like stroking your head and ears. I bravely put my hand near her head, determined that I would not pull away under any circumstances. If I did, the damage to my arm would be far worse. Pixie did her best not to let me down: she bit, dug in her claws, hissed, yowled and flared her nostrils in the most menacing manner she could. The girls at work examined the injuries on an almost daily basis whilst waiting with baited breath for me to get a photo of this demented animal so that they could see what was causing all this damage.

For the first month or so I would definitely say that Pixie won the battle, and my arm had the scars to prove it. Then one evening the teeth held my hand without digging in deep, so I dared to venture a little twitch of my finger across her head. I was quickly reminded which one of us was in control here. Another few weeks passed with similar battles of wills, and gradually I was able to stroke her for longer and with more and more of my hand. Pixie still hissed, but she didn't strike out or bite very often now, and when she did the damage was minimal. The nostrils had stopped flaring and the ears remained upright, so I decided it was time to introduce her to the other cats.

Pixie made it clear that she required nothing less than total respect from all other four-legged individuals, and returned to mustering her most menacing stance if one of the other cats dared look in her direction or – worse still – come within three feet of her. Attack first, ask questions later was her approach to all of them, and this ensured that she was given a wide berth by the other cats to avoid being on the receiving end of an unprovoked physical or verbal attack from her.

We all rubbed along fairly harmoniously for almost a year when suddenly Pixie decided to try out my knee. I was shocked, to say the least, when she jumped up, and I made the mistake of breathing which caused my body to move slightly, and she jumped down with a loud expression of displeasure.

Pixie was still on the homing list, and people came to see her with a view to offering her a new home.

'Oh, what a beautiful cat!' they would exclaim, then as they reached out to stroke her she would revert to her old ways and scratch or bite them or quite simply just hiss at them and they would add hastily, 'but she's not quite what we are looking for.'

By this time Pixie and I had reached an understanding: I could stroke her and pick her up for a cuddle – she would still hiss and yowl at me, but she never did me any harm. I had grown quite fond of her and her funny little ways and was prepared to accept her as she was, so she stayed with me.

The Cats Protection League run a sponsorship scheme for cats that are difficult to re-home, and it was suggested that Pixie should be a candidate for promotion under the scheme. I was asked to write a short article about her for the newsletter. An elderly lady decided that she wanted to sponsor Pixie and began sending in her monthly cheques to help pay for food and veterinary treatment. After a few months the lady asked for a photo of Pixie, and I duly produced one that I sent to her with a covering note to keep her up to date with Pixie's life. Then she asked if she could visit Pixie! Now, had it been any other cat I would have been happy to comply, but this was the highly-strung, temperamental, unreliable Pixie who had mauled other visitors coming to see her, and the lady concerned was in her eighties and therefore not very agile. However, she was determined to come and see the cat, so arrangements were made.

The day of the visit was sunny and warm and Pixie did not want to be kept indoors. Fortunately, to her credit Pixie always came when I called her, and as the visit was not taking place until the afternoon I decided that it was safer to let her out until her presence was required rather than risk having a bad-tempered cat forced to wait for a guest that she probably wouldn't want to see anyway!

I called her indoors about fifteen minutes before the lady arrived and made her wait in the downstairs hall while I helped the lady out of the car that had brought her and then down the pathway of the front garden.

I had put a chair in the hall, as I knew that the old lady would not be able to climb the stairs to my first-floor lounge. I helped her to sit down, aware that Pixie was watching the goings-on from the safety of the banisters. I encouraged Pixie to come downstairs, and with the normal huff, puff and howl she made her entrance into the hall and paced around the old lady's seat. I watched as the lady offered her hand to Pixie, and then held my breathe as Pixie's brain tried to decide what to do about this friendly gesture. She went a little closer and sniffed the extended hand and the lady stroked her head – Pixie immediately backed away with the usual hiss, but her curiosity was aroused, so she went back for another sniff and again the old lady managed to stroke her head, all the time talking to Pixie and receiving answers of a sort from this vociferous cat. Finally Pixie reverted to form and the paw came up to join the teeth around the hand. 'Pixie!' I said, in what I hoped was a controlled, warning voice, and she seemed to understand that this was not appropriate behaviour and released her hold on the undamaged hand.

'Oh dear!' said the old lady, 'she has had enough of being a good girl. She wants to go out, doesn't she? Let her go, I've had my stroke.'

Pixie shot out of the front door, but she stayed in the garden and chatted to the old lady as she made her slow progress back to the car. The visit was never repeated, but until she passed away a year or so later the old lady continued to send her monthly cheques to help Pixie.

One day Pixie went missing – and I was worried. I knew that it was most unlikely that this unfriendly cat had been picked up by strangers – they'd have soon put her down if anyone had tried to take her! Notices went up, neighbours were informed and I went out every night listening for her howls. My neighbours had gone away for a few days, so I went into their garden to check near their locked shed – surely this verbally expressive cat would respond if she were locked in their shed? Nothing. I tried this and other places again the next day and there was still no sight or sound of Pixie. I tried not to worry too much; after all, of all my cats this was the one most likely to be able to defend herself against foxes, dogs and humans, but I still could not stop thinking of her! My mind raced, I pictured her lying dead in the road (even though I had checked the roads) or under a bush, fatally injured – were there any bushes I hadn't checked?

On day four I went to work as usual and came home with a heavy heart, but as I opened the window to let the cats in and out I was greeted by a familiar howl and there was Pixie. As I showed her how pleased I was to see her, I heard a frantic knock at my front door – it was my neighbour.

'Your cat has been locked in my shed – I'm ever so sorry, I didn't realise she was there! She was ever so hungry and all I had was some ham and cheese so I gave her some of that!'

The moral of this story is that if your cat goes missing, even if you can open a shed door and call for them, don't assume that no response means the cat is not in there. I am sure that Pixie, who has normally got something to say about everything, kept quiet because she knew she shouldn't have been in the shed in the first place!

We moved house again and soon after the cats began to enjoy the pleasures of their new garden. I was aware that there were occasions when one of the local tomcats appeared to come in through our cat flap to steal food. I was glued to the TV screen one Saturday night watching the gory scenes on *Casualty* when I became aware of William moving from his spot by the kitchen radiator and thought he had become too hot.

Suddenly, *Crash! Bang! Wallop!* Arthur hurtled in through the cat flap and rushed upstairs and William, never very brave for all his size, leaped onto the windowsill, head poking out from behind the curtains. All the other cats suddenly came to life and crept towards the kitchen door. Like the three bears, it was a case of, 'Who's been eating my food, and is still there gobbling it all up?'

None of the cats seemed to want to chase off the intruder – except Pixie. Not known for her gentle nature and welcoming manner, she howled and bushed herself up to her biggest and most menacing size and quickly chased the interloper out through the cat flap again. The deed done, she huffed and puffed and snarled a few more times and then sat squarely in front of the cat flap, just daring him to come back in that way.

From that day on Pixie changed her habits and slept in the kitchen rather than in the lounge, one eye always open, just waiting for that big black-and-white cat to try and take her food again! In fact she realised that if she sat in front of the cat flap none of the other cats were brave enough to come in or go out, and this provided her with endless amusement. I would suddenly notice that there was a line of cats in the kitchen with their legs crossed waiting to go out, or a queue of cats on the patio trying to come in and I would have to make her move out of the way, hissing and spitting as usual, to restore normal traffic movement in and out of the house.

Fortunately Pixie has never really been ill in her life, and so her contact with vets has been minimal. When she has needed attention the vets have seen her as something of a challenge, and her loud howls and hisses under their hands have done nothing to calm the nerves of the animals waiting the other side of the consulting-room doors! However, she needed to go on one occasion and I braced myself for the battle ahead. She went into the basket fairly easily, and as the lid shut down on her I would say she was mildly cross. We got in the car for the short drive to the vet and got out at the other end, and by now Pixie was angry. There had been an emergency so we had to wait for an hour and Pixie did not like to be kept waiting – she was furious. When we finally got to see the vet, he was a locum (Oh dear!). I explained that she was not entirely happy.

'Don't worry,' he said, 'I relate well to cats.'

Pixie related well to him too: she had decided that he was the one person to blame for her present predicament and he looked nice and plump so she would have him for her tea. I left him to clear up the blood – his and mine – and I went home with a course of antibiotics. I'm not sure that either the vet or I knew what ailed Pixie or whether antibiotics would help, but I am certain that one or the other of us had saved face, somehow.

Twelve years later, she is still the same highly-strung cat, although the years have calmed her a little and we do now have some very tender, loving and close moments. Pixie has always wanted to be friendly, but her early experiences have never been forgotten and she can never relax enough to really enjoy these tender moments. The other cats still give her a wide berth, though, as she has not mellowed enough to stop her unprovoked attacks on them, and she still likes to sit in front of the cat flap daring any of them to pass her!

Chapter Nine

A Houseful of Cats – and a Window

S UDDENLY, THE NOISE OF PEOPLE SLAMMING CAR doors brought me back to the present, and as the car slowly moved out of the car park, I realised that I had been waiting for over an hour for Katy to appear. There was still no sign of her, so I poured myself a cup of coffee from the flask and settled back into the seat of the car with the comforting warmth of the cup held between my hands. I allowed my mind to wander back over the years, remembering some of the 'characters' who had shared my life for only a short space of time and yet had managed to secure a tiny, permanent piece of my heart.

When I first began cat rescue work I lived in a three-storey townhouse, and having no cat flap at the time the cats' preferred method of going in and out was via a middle-floor lounge window. Once on the windowsill it was just a short jump onto the protruding top of the integral garage roof and from there a short leap onto a fence and down into the garden. Posey never did manage the last part of this journey. She'd very bravely jump onto the garage roof, but the jump onto the fence was a little too scary for her – that fence was quite wobbly – so she used to play for hours on the roof, never daring to venture further.

In the summer the window remained open all day for cats to come and go, but in the winter it remained firmly closed until a loud howl would alert me to the fact that someone wanted to go in or out – or indeed simply wanted me to open the window so that they could see whether it really was as bad outside as they thought it looked!

Inevitably there were times when quite a few cats were lined up on the windowsill waiting to come in, and I was often aware of neighbours going up and down the road stopping outside my house to look at all the cats. The mothers with young children were the worst: they would stand on the pavement looking up at the window, and I would hear them say in rather loud voices, 'Oh, look at all the cats! How many can you see?' Then they would proceed to count: 'One… two… three…'

I am convinced that it is due to my love of cats that all those young children could count up to at least ten by the time they started school.

Over one hundred cats came in and went out via those windows – not all at the same time, but over a period of a few years. They stayed for a few days, weeks, months and even years sometimes before going on to new and loving permanent homes of their own, and sadly some of them spent their last days with me – hopefully having a happy ending to their lives.

Willow was living on the fifteenth floor of a block of flats in Bow, East London. I was working in Stratford at the time and went to collect him on my way home one evening; his owner had finally decided that the living arrangements were not suitable for a cat. Willow was white and tabby with wonky back legs – the result of an old injury that neither restricted him nor caused him pain; it just made him look a bit odd when he walked as his legs sort of wobbled like a jelly. He had a super temperament and loved to be stroked and was a real lap cat.

Just before he came to stay with me I had taken in a beautiful young calico tortie with a white stomach and legs. I had called her Rainbow and she had been found in a coal shed with her four kittens. I didn't ever see her kittens – they were all homed immediately – and I understood from the person who rescued them that all the kittens and

Rainbow had looked as though they were black they were so heavily covered in coal dust. By the time she came to me our excellent veterinary nurses had given her a clean up so she was back to her former colour and beauty – it was little wonder then that Willow swooned; he fell in love with Rainbow on sight, and the feeling was mutual! They came during the autumn and having gazed into each other's eyes they immediately became inseparable. They would lie in front of the fire in the evenings with their paws touching, gently licking each other from time to time. As I watched I couldn't bear the thought of them being homed separately, and I made a home together the criteria for them being re-homed at all.

My prayers were answered: a mother and her daughter who had been approved to adopt a pair of cats came to see Willow and Rainbow. They fell in love with them, and to my delight Willow and Rainbow appeared to approve of them too. After much purring and head-butting of hands and legs from the cats and much billing and cooing from the mother and daughter, I was reasonably happy to put the cats in baskets before they set off on the journey to their new home together.

Poor little Mitzi did not have such a happy end to her story. This dear little black cat had diarrhoea, so her owner threw her out to fend for herself rather than take her to the vet. She was elderly and had no teeth left so she didn't really stand much chance of surviving on her own. A member of the public had felt sorry for her and contacted the CPL, who in turn asked if I would help by fostering her. It was true to say that the diarrhoea was very bad, and despite giving her the dietary food recommended by the vet and then several powders and pills to try and curb the diarrhoea it was finally diagnosed that she had cancer, and after a week or two more – mostly spent in the garden enjoying the warmth of the summer sun – she was finally put to sleep. I hope she took some happy memories with her of her last few weeks of life.

Judy, a fat black-and-white cat, came to stay around the time of the first Gulf War when George Bush Senior was flexing his muscles against Sadam Hussein. Although she was quite a cuddly, friendly cat with me, Judy wasn't all that keen on the other cats. Her favourite sleeping place was under the settee, where she would lie in wait for any passing cats. As soon as she saw a set of paws she would, in one movement, rush out and attack the owner of the paws and then fly back to her unassailable 'bunker' under the settee. Needless to say, any 'thinking' cat in the house made sure that they gave the settee a wide berth after falling foul of a couple of these unexpected assaults.

She was nicknamed 'Scud' after the missiles used in the war in progress at that time, and this was how she was introduced to friends and family. Only prospective new owners were ever introduced to Judy by her proper name in case the nickname scared them off and they didn't offer her a home! She did eventually go to a home of her own after a few months and went off to a life of bliss with a single owner and no other cats to contend with.

One of my neighbours knocked on my door one evening in December. By now I was known locally as 'Cat Woman' – a title that has remained with me to this day.

'There's a lovely cat wandering up and down the street – she looks lost – what can we do?' she asked.

That was the royal 'we', of course, so I collected a cat basket and went off with her to meet the distressed cat. It was a lovely white-and-tabby cat, and as it was so close to Christmas I thought that Holly would be an appropriately seasonal name.

She really was a super cat, and I couldn't believe that there wasn't an owner somewhere going out of their mind with worry over her disappearance. The wheels of the CPL were put into motion; lost and found register keepers were contacted, an advert was placed in the local newspapers, posters were put up locally and door-to-door enquiries were made, but no one seemed to be missing Holly. I could only assume that being so friendly and human-orientated she had got into a van and been unwittingly moved from her own location to this new and strange area where she became just another lost cat – if only they could speak and tell you their stories!

Holly was on the homing list, and soon after deciding that her real owner was never going to materialise, one of the home-checkers contacted me as she was looking for a nice, gentle, friendly cat for a family that she had already visited and approved – would Holly fit the bill?

There were three nice little girls in the family aged five, seven and nine who had never had a cat before because the eldest child had been asthmatic from birth. Mum and Dad were confirmed cat lovers and had really missed having a cat in their family for the last nine years. The good news was that the daughter had now outgrown the asthma and the doctor had given the family the all clear to go out and get a cat.

Mother and daughters arrived to see Holly – Dad was a firefighter and had to work, so he had entrusted the four women in his life to decide upon the right cat for them.

The children were delightful, but very nervous of the cat and Holly seemed to know this instinctively. I could tell the mother was smitten already – I think she would have taken anything with four legs and a tail that went meow! She encouraged the eldest of her daughters to stroke Holly, and the child stretched out a tentative hand towards the cat, who simultaneously and slowly stretched out her head to meet the hand and very, very gently proceeded to lick it. This dissolved the younger children into squeals of delight, and they put their outstretched hands toward Holly, who gave each of them the same treatment – more squeals of delight! Holly was officially asked by Mum and each of the children in turn if she would like to go and live with them, and she appeared to purr her agreement, so she packed her bags and left me that evening.

I heard from the still-delighted family a week later. They assured me that Holly had settled into her new home, and even Dad had fallen in love with their new cat. All the children came on the telephone one by one to promise me that they would take very good care of Holly and say that they loved her very much already.

Muffin was a beautiful black cat with a white bib. She was about seven when she came to me after her owner went into respite care. She was obviously used to a great deal of attention on a one-to-one basis, and she hated other cats; imagine being a cat who hates other cats and then finding yourself landed in my house where there are at least ten other felines! Muffin liked me – she even loved me at times – but she hated those other four-legged furry things with tails; she didn't recognise them as being anything like her and she made their lives misery! She didn't differentiate between males and females; she'd have a go at any of them – especially if they were fast asleep in a chair, when she'd jump up and towering over her unsuspecting prey she would wake them by hissing, spitting and growling, baring her teeth like a dog while the object of her hatred cowered deeper into the chair cushion, too scared to move or fight back, hoping that I would be there to come to their rescue. I admitted defeat and asked all the home-checkers to make sure that Muffin was offered to the next suitable home that came along.

Luckily for all of us this was a single, middle-aged lady who wanted just one cat to keep her company as she began her early retirement from work. Fortunately Muffin proved to be just the right cat for her, and my 'family' were left alone to recover from Muffin's short but memorable stay with us.

I remembered dear little Polly who loved to sit on my windowsill in the sunshine. She was a pretty tortie tabby with white chest and legs who wanted to be stroked and petted, but she would suddenly turn and attack very aggressively. She was another cat who had diarrhoea quite badly, and again I found myself trying all manner of pills, potions and diets on her as recommended by the vet – all to no avail! In desperation one day I told the vet that I was sure there was something seriously wrong with Polly, and I thought that her aggressive behaviour only happened when I touched parts of her that were painful, so he decided to operate after morning surgery to see what was going on inside her.

He rang me later that day while she was under anaesthetic; she had cancer, so we agreed that Polly would never wake up – she was out of pain at last.

Poor little Danny had no fur when he was picked up and brought to my house. He was elderly and had been a stray for quite some time. We thought that regular food and warm shelter would see his fur growing back and his strength improve, but sadly this did not happen and it was finally discovered that he had a tumour which was inoperable, and after a little while he was laid to rest.

A white-and-tabby cat quite often visited my windowsill where he knew he stood a chance of being fed. I knew he wasn't neutered as my windowsill began to smell of tomcat, and despite efforts to try and find an owner locally, none appeared. He began to look a little dishevelled and grubby, and I made up my mind that I would try and catch him, get him neutered and find him a new home.

One day, when he came for his food on the windowsill I made a grab and in one movement this shocked little cat was scruffed and popped in a basket before he realised what was happening. He went to have his operation and then came home to spend a few days in the garden pen to recover. I called him Jimmy and I continued to try and trace an owner for the next few days.

After day four of being in the pen receiving regular food and the odd tasty morsel of chicken as a treat, I decided that the time had come for him to be released; he knew the area and would surely come to me all the time now that he recognised me as an ongoing provider of the essentials of life. I opened the pen door and we spent several minutes having a cuddle and stroke and then he casually walked along the sideway of my house, stopping once to look back towards me before continuing on his way. I never ever saw him again – he simply disappeared! Did he go back home? I really don't know – I had the whole street looking for him, but we never found him.

I could never forget the telephone call that heralded the arrival of twelve-week-old Bartie one Saturday afternoon.

'I've found a kitten,' said the voice. 'I can't keep him because I've got kids. Can you pick him up now?'

Something about the voice worried me, and the address she gave was in a notoriously bad area for any cat. It made me drop everything, pick up a cat basket from the garage and rush off to collect the kitten before it was handed out to some awful family who would tire of it in a couple of days.

It was a lovely hot summer's day, and as I parked the car in one of the allocated bays I looked around me and resolved not to leave a car window open despite the heat. The car park was filled with groups of men – young and old – all stripped to the waist, their sweaty bodies covered in tattoos, oil and grease as they worked on cars that looked as though they would never be roadworthy again – if indeed they ever were! Relieved that my car at the time was a ten-year-old rear-engine Skoda, I locked the door and went in search of the flat in the labyrinth of concrete buildings.

I rang the doorbell and after a few seconds the door opened and a head appeared round it, ring through nose, multi-coloured cropped hair and an enquiring and none too friendly expression.

'I've come about the kitten,' I said.

An arm appeared slowly from behind the door to join the apparently dismembered head, and as it stretched out, in the hand was a small black-and-white kitten. I quickly took hold of it and placed it into the cat basket on the doorstep. As I stood up, I barely heard the mumbled 'Thank you' as the arm and head disappeared into the darkness of the flat and the door was closed in my face.

I retraced my steps back to the car – thankfully it was still standing intact. The men, still bent over their car engines, gave me a cursory glance as I put the cat basket in the car and the kitten and I made our way back home. Bartie – I can't recall what made me choose that particular name for him – was re-homed after only a couple of days. Someone was waiting for a kitten to share their home and he was deemed suitable – nice, friendly kittens never seemed to stay with me for very long.

Fiver and Sweetie were related and already had their names when they came to me. Fiver was so-called because her owner sold her kittens at his garden gate and charged a fiver for them. She was a long-haired cat of brown and white colour and Sweetie (the name was very appropriate as she was just that: a sweetie) was white with black patches and an adorable little heart-shaped black patch on her nose. Fiver was up front and worldly-wise, but Sweetie was a really petrified little dear who absolutely idolised Fiver and followed her everywhere – so long as she could see Fiver everything was all right, but the moment Fiver disappeared from view you could see the panic starting to set in Sweetie's eyes. For this reason and the fact that they had always been together it was essential that these two cats were found a home together. It wasn't easy because Fiver was at least eight and Sweetie was about six, and prospective new homes always seemed to want younger cats. After two years of waiting I had almost given up hope and was in the process of making my mind up to keep these two very lovely cats.

I got quite a shock when suddenly a home popped up and arrangements were made for the couple, who had previously been home-checked and approved to adopt a pair of our cats, to come and see them. I explained that Fiver would settle immediately but that Sweetie would need a great deal of time and confidence-building before it would be safe to let her go out, but none of this was going to deter this very nice young couple from taking my two 'girls' to share their home. I received regular letters and photographs to show me how well they were settling into their new home and how it had taken much longer for Sweetie to accept her new owners and how she was still devoted to Fiver!

Whisky was ten years old when her owner died. She had lived in a flat since she was six weeks old and had never felt the grass beneath her feet or the rain on her fur or met another cat; imagine how she felt when she found herself in my menagerie! She was a nice old lady of a cat, all black and very obviously used to plenty of attention, and if she didn't get it she would use her very loud voice to howl at me until she got the attention she felt she deserved.

Whisky wasn't all that impressed by the other cats, and to avoid encountering any of them she travelled about the house trying not to touch the floor! From the table she'd jump onto the chairs, up onto the side server, across the Welsh dresser and onto the kitchen worktop for food. She would then reverse her journey to one of her favourite sleeping places. The only time she hit the floor was at bedtime, and then she would race upstairs as though the devil himself were after her.

As she showed no sign of being interested in the world outside I gradually felt relaxed about leaving the window open for the cats to come and go as they pleased, and one day I saw her sunning herself on the outside window ledge; she appeared to be quite happy sitting in the fresh air, so I left her to it, just keeping an eye on her to make sure she was still there.

Suddenly she was gone! I searched the house but there was no sign of her, and I really couldn't believe that she had gone outside, but as I looked into the garden there she was, tentatively exploring every bush and blade of grass. I went to the back door and tried to call her in, but she was determined to stay outside and I was worried that if I tried to grab her she would run away, so I left her to her own devices for a little while, and when I went to try and find her again she had disappeared.

I had the whole street looking for a black cat with no distinguishing marks – and I met hundreds of other black cats that I had never been aware of before in the area in the ensuing forty-eight hours. Then one of my neighbours said she thought she had seen her by some garages just up the road from me, and armed with a basket, I went to investigate. It was Whisky, but other than coming halfway towards me by way of recognition, this stubborn old cat had no intention of coming home with me now that she had found this new life outdoors! I went to get some food to try and tempt her with, and she must have been a bit peckish as she came to eat from the bowl I put down and I managed to grab her and push her into the basket. She put up quite a fight, and not for the first time I went home with blood pouring down my arms. As soon as I released her from the basket she rushed over to the window expecting it to be open – it wasn't – so she had to settle down and have some food and a good long sleep.

After that little experience of the big wide world Whisky

realised what she had been missing all her life, and although she never stayed out for so long again, she did spend most of her days rolling on the grass or sitting in the warmth of the sunshine, sheltering under one of the bushes in the garden when she became too hot.

I was delighted when a new home was found for her with a garden; a lady and her adult daughter wanted an elderly cat because they thought quite correctly that most people wanted young cats or kittens and they felt sorry for all the old cats who needed their own homes. They had taken in elderly cats from the Cats Protection League before, and the last of these had just passed away so they came to see Whisky, fell in love with her and took her home with them straight away. I heard from them a few weeks later and they said that Whisky had settled in well and seemed to be happy and she was now discovering the delights of her very own garden. She was becoming quite renowned locally for chasing off any visiting felines that dared to set paws on her land!

Fifi had a broken leg when she came to stay with me and she had to have complete pen rest for six weeks. She had fallen from a window and, faced with a large bill for veterinary care, her owners signed her over to the Cats Protection League for re-homing. Fifi was a lovely little tabby-and-white cat, not yet two years of age, and her hind leg was covered in plaster from the thigh down when I went to pick her up from the vet.

For the first week Fifi was happy to stay in the pen so long as she received plenty of strokes and food, but from the second week, having recovered from the shock of her ordeal, she thought that it was high time she was allowed out of her enclosure, and she meowed pitifully every time she saw me.

I began to take her out in the evenings and sit with her on my knee or next to me on the settee, and this seemed to satisfy her until week three. By this time she wanted to explore her new surroundings, and so I started to allow her a little gentle exercise for about ten minutes on the floor in the lounge; she couldn't really walk very well with the heavy plaster on her leg, but she was determined to try! By the time week four arrived she had overcome the lameness of her hind leg, and I spent the evening chasing around the room after her trying to make sure that she didn't jump or try racing up the stairs! By week five I was quite laid back and would sit and watch her as she gambolled around the room, but I still put her back in the pen when I was at work or going out, and she still objected loudly!

We both anticipated week six with relish and were delighted when that plaster came off and the broken leg was pronounced mended. Fifi came home and proceeded to wash her mended leg fervently and I took down the pen and put it back into storage. She was quite happy to spend the evening sitting on the settee with me, and at last she could explore the upstairs and downstairs of her new temporary home before she finally went to a new home of her own with one of our volunteers.

I was suddenly aware that there was a huge black-and-white cat in the neighbourhood and that he was terrorising all the local cats. Ziggy and Thomas both needed veterinary treatment after coming off second best following an encounter with him. Something had to be done, but what? He didn't appear to have an owner and he shunned food. He was nervous of humans and dominant of any other male cat who happened to cross his path and he quickly started to look as though he was 'living rough'.

One fine, sunny day I left the lounge window open for the cats to come and go and got on with my washing-up. I was suddenly aware of a fracas in the lounge and rushed in to see what was happening. There, in all his glory, was the big black-and-white cat. He ran downstairs, hotly pursued by me and the other cats. I thought quickly and realised this would probably be my only chance to catch him. I grabbed a towel and threw it over his head and quickly bundled him into the garden pen.

Whether through shock or relief that someone was finally going to look after him, Rambo meowed and rubbed himself round my legs. The scourge of the neighbourhood was no more than an extra outsize pussycat.

After a quick trip to the vet for neutering, Rambo returned to my garden pen to recover. He was allowed to join the household on a temporary basis following a few male supremacy disputes and a great deal of wheedling from Rambo himself. The name had seemed appropriate on account of his muscular frame, and his size would have made even Sylvester Stallone himself look like a weakling, but when I got to know Rambo he was really a gentle giant and loved nothing more than a cuddle and a knee to sit on.

An elderly lady and her middle-aged daughter had just lost their much-loved cat, and having passed the home-check they were told about Rambo and wanted to take him even though they hadn't seen him. I delivered him to his new home – a lovely bungalow with a huge garden backing onto a park. The two ladies were lovely – I couldn't fault either them or the home they were offering, so I came home alone. Leaving him there was one of the hardest things I have ever done, even though I knew beyond a shadow of a doubt that he would be loved and cared for throughout his remaining years.

Pansy was one of several cats taken in when the owner (who had a liking for black cats) went into care. She was semi-feral and hissed and spat when I touched her to begin with, but underneath that frosty exterior was a gentle little cat, as I was to discover. After a few months I recognised that Pansy would probably never be friendly enough to find another home, so she became another permanent resident.

Several years after her arrival I was able to stroke her and administer pills if she was ill, but never to pick her up and cuddle her or have her sleeping on my knee. She adored Posey and would wait until she was asleep when she would creep up onto the chair with her and sleep in absolute oblivion – when Posey was awake she didn't have time for Pansy's attentions; there was always too much to do!

I didn't really know how old Pansy was, except that she was a middle-aged cat when she first arrived, but I guess that she was over ten years old when I became aware that she was having problems eating, so I braced myself for a trip to the vet.

I warned the vet that there was little point in a consultation beforehand as they would have to sedate her to look at her, so I just took her down one morning thinking that she probably needed some teeth removed. I also warned them to treat her with the respect that they would a feral cat and went to work. I received a telephone call from the vet while I was in the office.

'Your cat has caused us a few problems,' said the vet. 'How do you manage with her at home? She is horrendous!'

What? My dear, sweet little Pansy – horrendous? The vet went on to say that they had removed teeth but also detected a mass in her mouth which they had removed but weren't very happy about. Would I be able to give her antibiotics, and did I want them to bring her round from the anaesthetic? Yes, of course I did, and I went to collect her later that day. Pansy had to be put in a pen for the next few days while treatment was ongoing, and five days later they wanted to see her back for a check-up.

'Even if we can only make her hiss, we may be able to see inside her mouth,' said the vet. Pansy and I duly attended the follow-up appointment, and this time we saw a rather nice young locum vet, John. I started to explain how bad she had been on the day of the operation and he stopped me in my tracks.

'I was there,' he said, and continued, 'I have never seen anything react as violently as she did – she was quite frightening!'

He watched me open the basket and pick Pansy up and hold her in my arms. I gently opened her mouth for him to look inside, and when he had finished I popped her back in her basket. She had not hissed or spat, nor did she struggle.

He followed me into the reception area and said to the nurses and the other vet who happened to be there, 'I've never seen anything like it; that horrendous cat was as good as gold, you wouldn't think it was the same animal!'

Several weeks later Pansy appeared to be having the same problems and there was a little watery blood coming out of her mouth, so we went back to see the vet – the same nice young vet called John. With me present, he was more confident around her this time – the news was not good, though. The mass they had removed from her mouth in the earlier operation was suspected to be a tumour, and it had grown again and was even bigger than before. We decided that there was only one course of action, and he took me into a side room where he gave her a sedative and left me with her for ten minutes or so to say my goodbyes before coming back to give her the lethal dose.

As I left with my empty basket John said gently, 'You know, that cat really loved and trusted you – I cannot begin to describe what she was like without you.'

Just before Christmas 1992 I collected two young cats from the vet where they had been spayed. One of the cats was on our homing list with a second cat that the owner no longer wanted, but they had to stay where they were until we had spaces for them. When I arrived at the house their owner greeted me with a child howling in her arms and two more children were yelling at each other in the hallway.

Another cat sat huddled under a table, and strewn all over the floor were toys, decorations and cat vomit which was obviously a few days old and had just remained where it had been deposited. A kitten ran between our legs and I just managed to retrieve it before it shot out into the road. I made my mind up on the doorstep that I would take whichever I could of the cats and foster them myself. The kitten and the newly-spayed six-month-old black cat were the ones she no longer wanted, so they came home with me that night.

The kitten was easily homed – with my goddaughter's family as they had just lost their elderly cat and they came to visit and took him home with them. The other cat, Blackie, was petrified and I could not get anywhere near her. For three months I forced her to be touched and it was like stroking a stone garden ornament – she would go absolutely rigid, only her big yellow eyes rolled in her head for fear of what I might do to her.

One night a call of nature woke me from my sleep, and whilst sitting on the loo of all places I suddenly found myself stroking a very excited and friendly black cat who meowed and purred around my legs. The next morning she had reverted to doing her impression of a stone cat again.

Having a very weak bladder, we managed to keep up these nocturnal liaisons for several months, and gradually I was allowed a stroke during the day. I'm not sure when our relationship really blossomed; maybe it was when she decided that I was totally incapable of serving up cat food without her help and supervision, or maybe it was when I found just the right spot to tickle on her very ticklish tummy, but we got on famously from then on. She is still very nervous of any visitors and the sound of a doorbell, even on the TV, will send her off like a rocket to hide in the bedroom or garden.

Blackie quickly found her spot on my bed at night, and

as I switched off the light in the lounge she would shoot upstairs to make sure that she was ahead of all the other cats to take up her night-time position. More and more of my bed was being taken over by cats!

If I had known that Blackie was going to stay with me forever, I would probably have given her a more imaginative name, but that was never the intention. It is very hard to home even the most friendly of cats, and when prospective new owners have to crawl under a bed to see the cat that is meant to be the cat of their dreams, it doesn't augur well, so Blackie remained with me and so did her name. She became a quite adorable little cat, still with a very ticklish tummy and one who still disappears whenever strangers are about.

All these cats and many, many more had come in and out of those windows during their stay with me, and as I recalled their faces one by one, I realised that each one had left me with a memory to cherish forever.

Chapter Ten

Sir George and Lady Katie

I RECEIVED A CALL FROM A YOUNG MAN LIVING ALONE who wanted to adopt a cat. One of my colleagues and I went to do the home-check together having decided that an older cat would be most suitable for someone out at work all day. We even had a cat in mind – providing he proved suitable to become an owner of one of our rescue cats.

As he opened the door, he said, 'Oh, sorry, I should have rung you, I've got a kitten from somebody at work.'

A little annoyed at such a waste of our time, we asked to see the kitten – a dear little tortoiseshell of about ten weeks. We immediately went into advice mode and discovered quite quickly that he had a kitten, yes, but no litter tray, no food and really no idea about how to look after any animal, let alone this single-minded little kitten.

Fortunately, he lived only a few minutes away from me, so home I went to collect all the necessary items to get him through the first twenty-four hours. Having deposited these essentials with him and left leaflets for him to read about rearing a kitten, I also left my telephone number and said that if he had any problems at all he should give me a call. That was Thursday evening.

He rang me on Friday evening – she wouldn't eat her food and she had kept him awake all night wanting to play. He rang me twice on Saturday – she had kept him awake again and she had not used her litter tray, preferring instead to use the bath (at least she tried to get the right room!) and again she had refused to eat the food he gave her. He rang me three or four times on Sunday with much the same problems, except this time she had added climbing up the expensive new curtains to her list of misdemeanours. On Monday evening he rang me again and said, 'I can't cope with her any more, can you come and take her away?'

I went straight away and collected this monster kitten and all the equipment that I had left with him. True to the tortoiseshell temperament, this tiny kitten jumped out of her basket in my lounge, arched her back, fluffed up her fur and informed all the other bemused adult cats that she had arrived and would not tolerate any grief from them, no matter how big they were. Then she immediately went to find out what the food was like in my house and scoffed a big plate of cat food, so I really don't know what food he had given her that offended her palate so much. She spent the night on my bed, sucking my little finger – just as if she knew that by doing this she was securing her permanent place in my home. Katie Kitten had come to stay – as if I hadn't secretly prayed for that from the first moment I saw her!

A week or two after Katie's arrival, one of my work colleagues wanted to go to the local pet shop at lunchtime to buy some bits for her own two cats. I went with her, although it was only my intention to go to the post office next door. Having done what I needed to do I looked for my friend and found her still waiting to be served in the pet shop. I went in to join her and that was my *big* mistake.

As I looked around the shop, my eyes fell first of all on an owl tethered to a perch and then on a pen full of tiny kittens of all colours. In the pen was one tiny litter tray that looked as though it hadn't been cleaned out for a week and one tiny food bowl which was certainly not of an adequate size for the nine or so kittens in the pen to eat from. I was horrified by the conditions that met my eyes.

I had always wanted a ginger cat, and three of the kittens

were ginger; two were light ginger and one a much darker ginger in colour. I asked the owner how much the kittens were and was told they were thirty pounds. I looked in my purse – I would have bought all of them if the money had been available.

'Please could I have a look at the dark ginger kitten?'

The kitten was picked up and put into my outstretched hands. There really wasn't any doubt, but I checked eyes and ears as carefully as I could under the watchful, and by now somewhat suspicious, eyes of the owner.

'I'll take this one, I'll pay for him now and will pick him up after work at four o' clock,' I said, handing over the cash.

I never thought I would ever be motivated to buy a kitten in a pet shop, and I admit that I felt a certain pang of guilt for encouraging this sort of trade.

Back at the office I first contacted the RSPCA and then wrote a letter to the Environmental Health Officer of the local council and finally contacted the local CPL branch complaining to all of them about the conditions I had found in the shop.

The kitten was picked up and taken home at the end of the working day. He protested vehemently at being in a box for the journey home and was very pleased when he came out at the other end, especially when he saw other cats and kittens. He rushed up to long-haired tabby Oliver and nuzzled into his fur. Oliver was very definitely not the type of cat that appreciated this sort of treatment from anyone, and he looked at this tiny ginger thing in total amazement before sidestepping over it and then carrying on with his dinner.

A very jealous Katie decided that she hated this new kitten as soon as she set eyes on him and hissed and spat at him. The kitten was unabashed by this display of ferocity, and deciding that she was more his size than any of the others, he chased after her like a shadow. When he played with her toys her annoyance really began to show, and she picked up every knitted mouse and ball in her mouth and took them, one by one, upstairs and out of his way. The kitten followed. He went upstairs quite well considering his tiny frame, but when he tried to come down he fell and tumbled down about the last six stairs. He didn't go near stairs again for quite some time after that, so Katie's toys were safe until he grew much bigger.

A name presented a problem. Marmaduke and Marmalade sounded too big for such a tiny creature. Hamish? Ginge? Tigger? Quite suddenly, the name came with the absent-minded singing of a nursery rhyme 'Georgy, Porgy, pudding and pie…' George was at last christened.

Several weeks later I received a call from a very pleasant RSPCA Inspector replying to my telephone call and letters. He and the Environmental Health Officer had visited the pet shop in question together. The owl was only being looked after by the pet shop owner while the bird's owner was on holiday. Unfortunately – or fortunately, as the case may be – there were no kittens for them to see in the shop on that visit, but he promised that they would be monitoring the shop from then on and would make sure that any future kittens for sale on the premises were being cared for properly.

'Did you buy anything?' asked the Inspector.

I could feel myself blushing as I said, 'Yes, I bought a kitten.'

The voice on the telephone laughed and then said, 'You're not the first and you won't be the last to do that.'

George's future was safe and secure, but I did wonder what fate had befallen the other kittens in the pen with him. Had they been as lucky?

George quickly settled into the routines of his new home and all the very large cats that he was to share his life with, although he was slightly bemused by Katie's unfriendly reaction towards him. I realised that he wasn't perhaps the brightest of kittens – in fact, I've always told George that when he was in God's line-up he must have been first in the queue for looks and at the end of the queue for brains. This manifested itself when I bought him his first toy – a furry mouse. There was a ginger one for George and a grey one for Katie. The latter pounced on hers as though she had been catching mice all her life. Amid great meowing and excitement she rushed down to the hall and proceeded to play. George looked at his mouse with a worried expression on his face; he didn't understand what had caused such a reaction from Katie, so he followed her downstairs to the hall to find out. Wrong move! Katie scolded her younger brother in no uncertain terms and chased him away from her 'trophy' immediately, running back upstairs with it held tightly in her mouth. George followed and looked at me with such a look of puzzlement on his face that I picked up his mouse and tried to show him what to do with it – he still didn't understand!

Fortunately for all of us – especially George – Katie wore herself out with all the excitement and running around, and after about half an hour she crashed out in her basket and went to sleep. George sniffed at both the mice – he still didn't understand what all the fuss was about.

George was a nightmare to feed; he just wasn't interested in food, and the slightest sound provided him with an excuse to leave his bowl and rush off to investigate whatever it was he had heard. He was happier if the food was in my hand rather than on a plate, and this was the painfully slow way in which I made sure that George had something to eat.

Katie was a pig! She would noisily shovel food into her mouth, all the while keeping one eye on George's plate, ready to rush over and edge him out of the way so that she could have his food too – George was only too happy to stand back and let her clean his plate for him.

When George and Katie were kittens they looked so cute. George was ginger and his fur was all spiked and bushy, and although Katie – a pretty brindle tortie with white bib and paws – was a few weeks older, her fur hadn't yet become sleek and she had ginger tufts which spiked up in much the same way as George's. In truth, they both looked a bit like a couple of toilet brushes! They were photographed from all angles and I proudly showed off my new kittens to anyone who couldn't move quickly enough to avoid my photograph album. One of my CPL friends went on holiday and sent a postcard addressed to Sir George and Lady Katie – I can only presume it was a friendly jibe at my infatuation with my youngsters!

On our first trip to the vet for vaccinations they were of a size when they could both go in one basket. We sat inside the door of the reception area and waited our turn to see the vet. Sitting opposite us was another proud mother with her two young tabby-and-white kittens. As other clients joined us their eyes first set upon the two kittens opposite.

'Oh, how sweet!' they would exclaim, and the other mum puffed up with pride until their eyes, wandering around the room, fell upon *my* precocious pair, who managed to drum up their most plaintiff meows and most alluring looks.

'Oh, aren't you absolutely gorgeous!' they all exclaimed, and within a few minutes I found myself surrounded by a throng of people all peering into my basket of kittens. This did not go unnoticed by the mum opposite, who tried desperately to attract some of the attention away from my side of the room. I was relieved when they called my name and we escaped to the safety of the consulting room – but I must admit to a little feeling of pride for my two beauties!

Even now, at ten years old, Katie still hates George and will growl at him if he dares to come within more than a few yards of her. At night she likes to sleep on my bed, and as I turn the light out I wait to see whether George comes upstairs. The low rumbling growl from Katie alerts me to his presence, and in the soft light thrown into the room from the street, I can just make out George's tail held high above the bed as he circles it trying to decide whether to risk being chastised by me and jump up on the bed to make Katie screech so satisfyingly. The whole scene is like watching a clip from *Jaws*, with Katie and me marooned on the bed and George's tail becoming the predatory fin of the shark swimming around the bed! Eventually George either gets bored with Katie's growling and goes downstairs leaving us to get some sleep, or he manages to avoid my arms and scares Katie by jumping up on her in the dark.

Despite their advancing age they are both in good health, although George lost all his teeth at an early age, and he has now mastered the feat of playing with mice – either toys or real ones – but sadly for me he always brings the latter indoors to show me, and they are nearly always still alive!

Chapter Eleven

Bingo!

I WAS DOING THE IRONING WHILE THE SUNDAY JOINT was cooking slowly in the oven when the telephone rang.

'Sue, I need your help to trap a kitten, I've tried everyone else,' said the rather hysterical voice at the other end of the line.

Just what I needed! I turned the oven down to low and, hoping that the lamb would not be burned by the time I got back, got into the car and went to meet my colleague. The kitten had been spotted running around near a busy main road in south-east London.

We collected a trap on the way to our destination – a bingo hall that had an alleyway running all around it. On arrival we searched for the kitten, and suddenly we saw it shoot down the alleyway towards the rear of the bingo hall. I have to say that trapping was never my strong point, and I did wonder whether we would ever manage to catch the kitten, which was obviously scared to death. We needed a plan. We decided that we would set the trap near some bins and then try and herd the kitten towards the area. The trap was baited with pilchards in tomato sauce – recognised by experienced trappers to be the one thing that almost guarantees the capture of even the most ferocious feral cat – and whilst I waited by the trap, hidden from view but still able to see it, my colleague approached the kitten from the other end of the alleyway, trying to make it run towards the trap. Things were going well until a car backfired and the kitten, who had been gingerly approaching the desired area, suddenly turned tail and ran for cover under some boxes piled up in the alleyway.

We decided between us to have a break for a few minutes to let the kitten calm down, after which my colleague once again tried to coax the kitten into moving in the direction of the trap, this time with more success. The smell of the pilchards at last got to the nostrils of the kitten, and carefully she stepped just inside the trap to taste the morsel of pilchard near the door. My heart rate increased. I knew that if I pulled the string too quickly she would have time to get out of the trap before I could close the door behind her. I thought of the lamb roasting at home and waited and watched for one second, then another, and then suddenly I pulled the string and with one loud *Slam!* I had pulled the door shut and the kitten was inside the trap. We secured the trap door and put kitten and trap into my car – everything smelled of pilchards!

Once home I was able to assess what I had caught: a kitten of about ten to twelve weeks old and probably born wild. She had little fur on her body, but the tufts that remained visible indicated that she was tabby and possibly long-haired. She was alive with fleas and badly in need of a clean up, so I took her to the sink and filled a bowl with water and plonked her in. The water quickly turned red. I dried her off and rang the vet. Fortunately the nurse on duty knew me quite well and I was able to take the kitten down to them, even though it was Sunday afternoon by now. They discovered that although most of the 'blood' was from flea dirt, the poor little mite had an enormous abscess on her bottom, so she was sent home the next day with a course of antibiotics after a de-flea and general clean up.

Bingo, as I named her, was not an easy kitten to deal with. She did not hiss, spit and growl as feral kittens usually do, but by crouching in the furthest corner of the pen from me she made it obvious that she resented any kind of contact with me. She had to be restrained in a kitten pen for the duration of her course of antibiotics, otherwise I would have spent long hours trying to catch her to administer drugs. With this enforced captivity, regular food and medical treatment her fur began to grow back and fluff up. From an ugly duckling she transformed into a real chocolate-box, long-haired tabby, with an exceptionally beautiful tail. Unfortunately she remained untouchable – not vicious, but nevertheless she did not want hands-on contact with me or anyone else.

The day came when Bingo finally had to be released from the pen; she had been in it long enough, and her medication finished I knew that she was never going to be friendly enough to re-home and that she would join my increasing family of cats.

A week or so after we had trapped Bingo another of my CPL colleagues told me that a call had been received about a colony of approximately thirty feral cats and kittens that were living behind the same bingo hall in south-east London. I couldn't believe it as we had seen no other cats in the area, and we would surely have noticed a colony of thirty cats! The situation became clearer over the next few days. At the back of the bingo hall there was a very high brick wall and the colony lived in the undergrowth above that brick wall. We think that Bingo may have jumped or fallen from the wall, and being so small did not have the strength to jump back up to her family.

Over a period of time the colony were all trapped and neutered, the kittens re-homed, and some eight or nine years later there is a very kind lady who goes to the site every night to feed the six remaining adult cats who had been neutered and returned to the site as they were young and too wild to be found new homes.

Bingo fell in love with George during her incarceration in the kitten pen. Every time he walked passed she would go to the side of the pen and mew softly to him: George took absolutely no notice whatsoever. As soon as she was allowed out of the pen the first animal she sought out was George. By now her tail had bushed up like a fox's brush, and as she rubbed her head around him, her erect tail was fluffed up to its fullest extent and beauty. Still George took no notice, in fact he appeared to be slightly irritated by this display of affection. The one George really wanted was Katie, and she was having none of him.

Bingo's unrequited love has continued throughout her life, and she has never had a kind word from George – yet still she adores him! If George comes in via the cat flap I can be sure that the cat flap will bang again and there will be Bingo, rushing up to George as though she is seeing him for the first time. After a quick nap George will go out again via the cat flap, and suddenly Bingo is no longer tired and rushes out to join him. George ignores her totally and sets his sights on Katie – with the usual rebuff. Poor Bingo! What must go through her mind when she sees George's affections being lavished upon Katie who is not in the least appreciative of all his attentions? It doesn't appear to discourage her from trying though, and sometimes, when George is asleep in a chair, she manages to squeeze in beside him without waking him up, and then she nuzzles her nose into his fur and makes the most of the closeness they share for those few minutes.

I had always wanted a bird table in the garden, so when we moved to a more rural location I bought one but resolved that should the casualties be too great it would be dispensed with or passed on to someone else without a resident cat. I bought a three-feet-tall stone statue of St Francis of Assisi with a bird on his shoulder, another at his feet and one more in his hand, and I placed that at the foot of the bird table, entrusting him with the safety of all who fed on it.

At first the bird table caused a great flurry of excitement among the cats, especially when a flock of starlings landed on it and fought amongst themselves over the scraps I had put out for them, but despite constant attempts not even Arthur managed to catch anything. Then the magpies moved in too and the cats began to lose all interest.

Bingo loved that bird table almost more than she loved George. She would spend most of her time sitting under it looking up. She wasn't actually interested in the birds, but she soon realised that tasty morsels of sausage were quite often dropped over the edge by the starlings as they squabbled over the food, and she would gobble up any delicacies that they rejected. The magpies were in the habit of doing the same thing, and quite often a scrap would erupt between one fluffy tabby cat and a magpie over which one of them was going to have one particular piece of food from the bird table above their heads. The birds became quite accustomed to seeing her there and didn't see her as a threat – the other cats rushing up the garden trying to appear invisible sent them flying off into the trees!

The squirrel soon discovered the bird table and the nuts I put out. Bingo hated that squirrel – and the feeling was quite mutual! The squirrel would enter the garden via the roof of the garden shed, from which vantage point he could see where that darned cat was hiding. If the coast was clear, he would leap across to the top of the table and proceed to eat whatever delicacies the birds had left for him. Bingo would always know he was there, and as soon as he saw her appear he would race down from the table, across the garden and up the side of the shed to the roof with Bingo in hot pursuit. I always wondered why he didn't just leap from the bird table to the shed roof, and can only presume that these crazy races with that cat were a source of amusement to him. From the shed roof the squirrel would look down on Bingo with a fist in the air, shaking it vigorously at her and shouting all manner of abuse before scampering off to the safety of the trees.

The bird table has remained in use and various birds have visited it over the years with very few fatal casualties. I have been surrogate mother to several magpies, starlings and pigeons over the years and all have survived. Cats and birds appear to have learned to live with each other in harmony in my garden – which I like to attribute to the watchful eye of St Francis – despite a few near misses when the birds have become too relaxed for a moment! I think that my cats are too lazy and well fed to want the bother of trying to catch birds – I just wish I could say the same for the mouse population, who appear to be a far easier takeaway meal.

Bingo remains as untouchable as the day she arrived and has to be trapped before going to the vet. Once there she is completely docile, but she curls up into a tight little ball like a hedgehog, and the vet and I literally have to prise her open to examine any part of her. If she needs on-going treatment I am afraid that the pen has to come out again for a few days. I wish that I were able to tickle her tummy or stroke her sumptuous fur – especially that wonderful tail – but the only time she will willingly allow any physical contact between us is when I have chicken for supper, and as I distribute the pieces amongst the cats her soft, fur-padded paws will gently clasp my fingers as she takes a tasty morsel into her mouth!

Chapter Twelve

Just William (or a Boy Called Lucy!)

I ADMIT THAT I WAS FEELING BROODY, SO WHEN THE telephone call came to go and have a look at a ginger kitten on my way home from work, I couldn't wait and rang the number immediately: no reply. Constant attempts to try and make contact with the person reporting the kitten failed – nobody answered for the entire weekend, during which time I had thought of William as a name for the kitten and already decided he was mine. I have a particular penchant for anything ginger! Monday evening came and went with still no response, so I gave it one last try on Tuesday, and this time I had success.

'Oh, sorry, I've been to spend the weekend with my mother,' said the voice at the other end of the telephone.

I arranged to pop in that afternoon – I couldn't wait for the day at work to end so that I could at last see my ginger kitten. I rang the doorbell and after a few minutes a young girl in her early twenties with a toddler in her arms opened the door. After the introductions were made she invited me in.

'The kitten is in here,' she said, opening a door to what I presumed was the lounge. 'I've called her Lucy, and she's lovely but rather too lively to have in this flat.'

She continued to tell me how she had found the kitten running around on a busy main road nearby. She had tried to find an owner but nobody seemed to know anything about it.

Finally, my eyes set upon the kitten – and what a beauty!

I picked him up and had a closer look; William's maleness was very evident – even at about fifteen weeks of age. When I corrected her sexing abilities the girl said, 'Oh dear! And I called him Lucy! No wonder he was so naughty – he was probably objecting to being called a girl!'

William was put into a basket and made the trip to his new home where he made his presence felt in very rough, boyish ways. The first week of his stay saw him rushed to the vet as an emergency one evening. He had been playing and rushing around the house like a lunatic up on the chairs, the banisters and finally the table. This was where he came unstuck, as he slid straight across the table and off the other side, landing awkwardly and heavily on a wooden bench. He ran away and hid under a chair – that hurt! Within a very short space of time a large lump appeared on his shoulder, and I thought he had dislocated something, so off we rushed to the vet. He had banged himself so hard that he had caused a mass of blood to build up which produced the lump – he was beginning to look like Quasimodo. The vet assured me that the lump would eventually disperse and he would be back to normal.

'Keep him quiet – don't let him get into any rough and tumbles,' said the vet. What she didn't tell me was how to stop him!

Rapidly approaching his first birthday, William was beginning to take his first bold steps into the outside world under the watchful eye of his mother. Imagine my horror when, on one of these sorties, I saw my beloved youngest son, tail bushed and on his belly, being threatened by a large black cat with tail equally bushed and back arched ready to attack. But I had no need to be alarmed, as George suddenly appeared from nowhere and put himself squarely between William and the black cat. George glanced casually over his shoulder a few times until William had retreated to the side of the house and then he saw off the adversary with a certain amount of relish. A few minutes later William and 'big brother' George were cavorting on the lawn, all danger forgotten – this time!

William grew into a big, fat cat of over one stone in weight, even though he was not the greediest of my cats by a long stretch. When we moved house and had to have a new cat flap installed, my friend, who did all the work for me, was highly amused by the fact that William was the first of my cats to be pushed through the hole in the door to test whether the aperture was 'William-sized.'

His weight and strength did not make matters easy when we needed to go to the vet. I used a white wire basket for all the other cats, but William had to have his own basket, a huge wicker one. He would go in easily enough, but once at the veterinary surgery we would have the devil of a time trying to get him out. On one occasion, as I was struggling with my head in the basket trying to unhook his claws which had a tight hold on the wicker basket, the obviously highly amused veterinary nurse said, 'Oh look, William! Your mummy's trying to get in the basket with you.' I failed to get him out so the vet had a go.

'Oh look, William!' said our comical nurse, 'now the vet is trying to get in the basket with you.'

We managed between us to haul a stone's worth of cat out of the basket and onto the consulting-room table. William slid across the table and gripped onto the edge of it with his front paws as though his life depended upon it, and once again we had to try and prise him off so the vet could check him over. Then came the words that I was hoping not to hear: 'Let's put him on the scales,' said the vet.

'Oh dear, William,' I said, 'this is the moment we've been dreading.'

The vet's eyes went from me to the cat and then back to me again, before she said, 'Don't worry, he's just big boned!'

I laughed as I replied, 'That's what I keep telling him!'

Fortunately, William's weight hadn't increased so he was allowed to go back in the basket – he rushed in as far as he could go and all you could see was one very large ginger bottom as he hid his head under the towel which was meant to be covering the bottom of the basket.

I came downstairs one morning and was alerted to William's odd behaviour in the lounge. I tried to ignore what he was doing and began the daily task of providing bowls of food for cats who, after much ado during the preparation, would rush to the bowls, sniff, look at me as though I were Dr Crippin and then walk away in disgust. This ritual over, I went upstairs again to shower and dress.

William and his antics still bugged me some thirty minutes later. Was there something alive under the trolley? I armed myself with broom and footstool to stand on – no mouse was going to run up my legs – and bravely moved the trolley with one outstretched arm. Something shot out rapidly and hid between the open door and the wall with William in hot pursuit. I moved the door and again something shot out, this time from under the door but too quickly for me to register which way it went. From my perch on top of the footstool I took a quick look around and gingerly moved a litter tray, a bag and the chair. No sign of movement. Suddenly, I heard a squeak from the kitchen and as I cautiously peered around the doorframe, several cats were sniffing under the washing machine.

I resolved to get on with my business. Fortunately that meant I was going out for a few hours. Surely by the time I came home the mouse would have been caught and I would find the body dead on the floor, either in the house or out on the patio? Either way, I could not move the washing machine to force it out, even had I been brave enough to do so.

Several hours later I opened the front door and walked into the lounge, carefully checking the floor for dead bodies. Nothing. I began to relax a little as I walked into the kitchen – nothing there either, not even a cat. *Problem resolved*, I thought to myself, and on a pleasant, late summer afternoon I decided to spend what remained of the day gardening.

On one of my tea-making trips indoors I was aware of William stretched out on the floor of the kitchen – probably because he was lying across the back door, and being rather large it was a bit like climbing Ben Nevis each time I had to step over him! My eyes glanced at the cooker clock; it was a quarter past three.

An hour or so later a call of nature took me indoors again, and by this time several cats had joined William in the kitchen. I tried to calm myself with the thought that it was nearly time for tea and this was the advanced guard. I heard a squeak and immediately jumped on the footstool. As I looked the mouse was daring an escape from under the washing machine. Minnie had seen it too – what a great game this was, a mobile mouse with none of the usual string attached! The mouse retreated to the comparative safety of the washing machine. Minnie quickly got bored with waiting and watching and she wandered off, but William remained at his post.

I put out bowls of food, but no one showed much interest. George joined William by the washing machine and other cats casually sniffed the gap under it as they walked past, no doubt some of them wondering what all the excitement was about. Katie seemed quite interested, but the closeness of both George and William, her arch-enemies, discouraged her from investigating further, and she decided to leave them to whatever it was that was going on.

Finally Arthur, the only truly gifted hunter in the house, decided to return home for dinner. It was by now seven o'clock in the evening, and as he entered the kitchen he quickly assessed the situation: nothing to be done here at the moment, so he turned his attention to the bowls of food and then sauntered into the lounge where he jumped onto the settee and curled up into a tight little ball to sleep. George and William continued their vigil in the kitchen.

There were occasional noises from the kitchen and each time I would see Arthur's ears twitch slightly and I knew that he was aware of the situation, despite appearing to be fast asleep. Another scuffle a little later and he went out to have a look, only to return five minutes later to take up his position on the settee.

At nine o'clock things really began to hot up, and Arthur suddenly woke up and shot to the kitchen. I peered around the doorframe to see George and William each covering one side of the washing machine with Arthur in between them covering any escape from the front. I sat in the lounge and listened. Fifteen minutes later there was quite a commotion and several squeaks, and then I heard the cat flap bang three times as Arthur, followed by George and William, took the mouse out onto the patio.

I sat and relaxed for the first time that day. Once more the cat flap banged three times as the heroes of the day came in, Arthur first, all fluffed up with pride at a job well done, then George and William (who for once had managed to stay awake all day), both of whom were totally shattered by their long vigils in front of the washing machine. The mouse was now dead on the patio and they could at last find a nice comfy chair to fall asleep on.

As he grew into adulthood William became a very laid back cat who did everything at one of two speeds: slow and stop! He took things in his stride, especially the unprovoked attacks from Pixie, but one day the worm turned. He was minding his own business stretched out on the patio one hot summer afternoon when Pixie walked past – she just could not resist having a swipe at him as she did, but she got more than she bargained for! Just as quickly, William struck back and chased her indoors where a very noisy squabble ensued – one that I had to stop. For once in her life someone had answered back, and Pixie did not like being on the receiving end of an attack. William received a great deal of respect from Pixie from then on; he only had to look in her direction and she would run!

William has become a favourite in a house where the word 'favourite' has been banned. On a cold wintry evening, there is nothing nicer than having this extra outsize cat sitting sprawled across your knee feeling the warmth from his body. I also love to watch him walking down the garden as he returns home from one of his tours of his domain. His body sways rhythmically as he strolls along the pathway and then, as he sees me watching from the kitchen window, the slow ambling gait turns into a gallop as he rushes down the steps and in through the cat flap, meowing with pleasure at the thought of seeing me and in anticipation of the warm welcome that his homecoming will receive.

Chapter Thirteen

Arthur, a Truly Magical Cat!

O N ONE OF MY NUMEROUS TRIPS TO THE VETERINARY surgery I was accosted immediately upon my arrival by two veterinary nurses and dragged off into the recovery room to see what had arrived in the past hour. A tiny black kitten was thrust into my arms and I was told that he had arrived in a basket from a local pet shop with another kitten that had died en route. As I adjusted the kitten in my arms, one of the nurses said, 'Oh look, you're bonding.'

This was followed by a tirade of chatter.

'We want you to foster him – he can't go home with you yet as we have to make sure he is eating. Look at the way he eats.'

At this a great pile of mixed kitten food was put in a saucer and the kitten was placed in front of it. His mouth opened like a lion's jaw and hovered over the mountain of food before closing over it and taking some into his mouth. By this time Laura, the vet, had joined the circle of people watching this tiny little kitten devouring his food.

'We don't know yet whether he will make it or not,' she said. 'We think he is about five weeks old and not really weaned properly. There could be all sorts of problems, but we'll keep him here and see how he goes.'

For the next two or three weeks I received almost daily bulletins on his progress. The nurses had taken it in turns to take him home with them for evenings and weekends so he wouldn't have to spend long, lonely hours in the surgery. In fact, it transpired that the kitten spent most of its days being cuddled – as soon as one nurse put him back in his pen another nurse got him out and had another cuddle, and he spent quite a lot of time welcoming clients whilst being held in one pair of arms or another in the reception area.

Finally the telephone call came: Arthur, as he had been christened, was ready to go. I went to collect the kitten straight away, and as he was brought to me, I found myself once more surrounded by vets and nurses.

'We've called him Arthur – you won't change it will you? We want you to keep him, don't re-home him – we want to see how he grows... he likes plenty of cuddles... you will keep him, won't you?'

I eventually managed to extricate myself from the group and home I went with a basket and one still tiny kitten, and it soon became obvious that Arthur had not enjoyed all the attention he had received at the hands of the veterinary staff. I picked him up to have a cuddle and welcome him to his new home and immediately his paws stretched out against me and he struggled to get down. He wanted to explore his new home and here was another silly female wanting to be all soppy. He grizzled and struggled, so I popped him down on the floor and watched as he went racing around the house investigating all the furniture and the other cats. It must have been very daunting for such a tiny kitten to be confronted with all those big cats, but Arthur didn't appear to care. It was a long time before he would let me have a real cuddle again!

A week or so later we went back to the vet for his first injection. Once again Arthur was subjected to cuddles from each of the nurses who discussed the changes in him in that short space of time. Only three weeks until the next visit for his second injection and more cuddles – poor Arthur!

As the weeks passed I noticed something strange. Was it my imagination, or was Arthur's tail changing colour? I noticed it especially when he was play-fighting with one of the other cats and trying to look menacing. He would bush up his tail, which now appeared to be white rather than black. I then noticed some white hairs appearing elsewhere on his coat. We went back for his second injection, and as he sat on the table in the consulting room Laura, the vet, looked at him and said, 'What have you done to him? He's gone white!'

At this point we were joined by a throng of nurses, all pointing at his tail and the other white hairs on his body, which, I have to admit, were very visible by now.

'I've never seen anything like it,' said the vet.

Other vets at the practice who had known Arthur were called in to have a look at this phenomenon. I began to feel as though Arthur's apparent colour change was entirely my fault rather than an act of nature. I lamely tried to blame it on the veterinary staff for naming him Arthur, as everyone knew that the Arthur in the cat food advert on television was a white cat! I was pleased to go home that evening with my little black kitten – or should that have been white kitten?

Several weeks later all Arthur's white fur miraculously began to disappear and he once again became black, apart from two white hairs on his chest, which remain until this day. Fortunately, I can prove all these events, as a friend of mine came and took photos of Arthur with his super professional camera and there, quite clearly displayed, is Arthur's white tail captured for posterity on film. I presented the vet with an enlarged and framed copy of the picture, and I am quite sure that both of us have dined out on the tale of this magical little kitten and his colour changes.

I was puzzled. On a dry, sunny Saturday in early spring how did Arthur manage to come home wet up to his knees and elbows? Having registered the thought I carried on with my chores. There were more pressing things to occupy my mind like hoovering and washing.

These tasks eventually done, I settled down in an armchair for a well-deserved cup of coffee.

Suddenly my peace was shattered by a loud wail. Cats heads looked up from their slumbers, one eye opened for a second before going back to sleep. Then another long, high-pitched wail. This was enough to make the cats move, and they all went off to investigate. Another loud wail and even I got up from my chair – was it a cat in distress?

As I approached the hall something moved and at least six cats formed a circle around it. Another howl and paws immediately stretched out, at which yet another howl hit the air. There, in the middle of the circle of cats, was a frog, or maybe a toad – I'm not sure which – and every time a paw dabbed at it, it howled loudly.

I armed myself with wastepaper basket and newspaper and bravely went to help him – aided and abetted by umpteen cats. I got him outside, released him behind the shed and went back indoors, only to find all my silly cats still searching the hall for the frog or toad that they were sure must still be there somewhere.

Arthur sat watching the antics with a satisfied expression on his face that seemed to say, 'Gosh! That was fun for everyone. Even Mum enjoyed that game.'

Sadly for me, he has tried to provide the same family entertainment on several occasions since that day – not always with the same prey.

I became convinced that Arthur suffered from nightmares – perhaps he had dreams of being confronted by a giant mouse intent upon destroying him, I really don't know – but he would wake up from a deep sleep and rush over to me, desperate to climb onto my knee for comfort until he had regained his courage and was sure that nothing was after him.

Arthur has grown into a small but stocky little cat with a definite strut in his stride. However, for a male he is a little coward and will rush indoors with his fur all bushed out when he is approached by an unknown and threatening tomcat, but his prowess as a hunter cannot be denied – just so long as his prey is much, much smaller than him!

Chapter Fourteen

A Tale of Three Kittens

'HUBBLE, BUBBLE, TOIL AND TROUBLE,' I MUSED, AS I watched three conspiratorial work colleagues walking past the office window, and I suddenly realised that I had found names for three little feral kittens that had been delivered into my safe keeping the previous night.

Hubble was black and white and the only male; he was also the least ferocious of the trio, and so I set my sights on taming him first. It only took a day or two of cuddles and strokes before he was allowed out of the kitten pen and delivered into the fatherly paws of Ziggy, who would teach him all that a boy cat needed to know.

Bubble was going to be tougher. She looked just like a Siamese in colour and markings – she even had dark blue eyes that would stay with her through adulthood. She used those eyes to good advantage when she wanted to scare me off and stop me picking her up: she would scowl at me from under her cat eyebrows, daring me to come any nearer. It took a week of forced handling and stroking – she made a very good attempt at resisting me – before I had a major breakthrough; I felt her body weaken slightly to me scratching her ears followed by a very slight, rumbling purr and I knew I had won the battle! A week later she went to her new home with one of our own fosterers who would carry on the work I had started with her.

Trouble was by far the most aptly named of the kittens. A short-haired tabby, she refused to allow herself to weaken and succumb to my constant attempts to touch her and maintained her very violent attitude towards me. The only person who could get her to reveal her nicer side was George my ginger cat, and Trouble loved him. I decided that she would be another cat that joined my household and that she had spent too long in the pen. Upon her release the first thing she did was make her way to George's side, and there she remained for the next three years.

Hubble – having lost one sister to a new home and given up on Trouble – had befriended Lizzie, another kitten of similar age who had come to stay, and the pair of them would play endless games together, racing around the house. Hubble had, by this time, decided that Ziggy was his hero. He wanted to copy everything that Ziggy did, but much as he tried there was one thing that Ziggy could do that he just wasn't big enough to copy: Ziggy would lie along the back of the armchair on his stomach with one front and one back leg draped over each side. Hubble's legs just weren't long enough, but it didn't stop him trying and falling off at every attempt!

I thought it would be rather nice to find a home for Hubble and Lizzie to share together, and when a friend of mine at work lost her own cat due to kidney failure I couldn't believe my luck! After a week or so I broached the subject of another cat – or kittens – and although neither she nor her husband, Jack, were opposed to the idea, Joan was going to Australia to see her daughter over Christmas and couldn't think about new additions to the family before then. This was a slight problem, so I thought about it for a few minutes before gathering together a couple of photos, one of each of the kittens. Then I got a notelet and wrote the following message:

'Dear Aunty Joan and Uncle Jack,

Our foster mum says that you are going to Australia soon, but she is prepared to look after us until you return if you would promise us a new home! We are really nice and would be ever so good if we came to live with you.

Lots of love, Hubble and Lizzie.

P.S. We enclose photos so you can see how beautiful we are.'

I put the photos and the note in an envelope, popped Joan's name on the front and then put the envelope in her pigeonhole at work for her to collect with the rest of her mail later that day. I heard no more until the following day when I met Joan outside the building.

'You are terrible!' she said.

She had taken the note home and left it on the kitchen table. After several hours Jack suddenly said to her, 'Are we having these kittens, or what?'

Jack was not joining her on the trip to Australia, so the kittens were delivered to them that weekend!

On her return from the holiday I heard all about the kittens and their development and how Jack was besotted with them. Joan told me that even their neighbours were amused by Jack's apparent infatuation.

'We never heard Jack talk to your kids the way he talks to those cats!' they had said laughing.

A little while later Joan was telling me about Hubble and one of his latest antics.

'That cat is just so funny,' she said. 'Last night he got up on the back of the armchair, and he was lying on his stomach with two legs draped down one side and the other two draped down the other – he looked so odd!' At last, Hubble's legs were long enough to copy Ziggy – he had not forgotten his hero!

Trouble still refused to let me within anything less than three feet of her, but she remained in my house for the next three years, during which time she never attempted to go outside – even when the window was open during the summer. Then one day she suddenly decided to venture out into the garden, and this was when her troubles really started as I couldn't get her back indoors. Even though I left the window and the doors open, she didn't have enough intelligence to find her way back indoors – she wouldn't even follow her much-adored George into the house.

Gradually, one by one the other cats began to turn on her and chase her from the garden. First the females gave chase, and when I fed this poor little tabby I had to shut the other cats indoors so that she could come and get her food. The males – even George – then started and were quite ferocious in their attacks upon her. The day came when I could cope no longer – I felt so sorry for her; this was the only home she had known and suddenly she was no longer welcomed. Why?

With the help of a friend I managed to trap her and get her into a basket. I took her to the vet. All advice sought had not worked and the situation was getting worse and Trouble herself was becoming more distressed by the day. She was put to sleep. As she lay on the table in the surgery, I stroked her poor limp body and said to the vet, 'In the three years of her life with me, this is the first time I have really been able to touch her – I feel as though I have let her down.'

He put an arm around my shoulder and said that he thought I had done the right thing. 'Imagine what an awful end she might have had if you had carried on with the situation as it was. What would you have done had she become ill – would you have been able to catch her then? Would the other cats have finally driven her right away to fend totally for herself, and would she have survived that?'

I knew that he was right and that I had made the right choice, but I still can't help feeling that somehow I failed that poor little tabby called Trouble.

Chapter Fifteen

Porky the Menace...

LATE ONE EVENING I WAS ASKED TO TAKE IN A STRANGE-looking beige cat that had just been caught. I began preparing the utility room wondering what on earth was coming into my home. I was soon to find out, and imagine my surprise when the basket that came through my front door produced my latest foster cat – a Pedigree Red Burmese! He even had a collar on with a telephone number on it; I dialled it but the number was unobtainable. It was now late at night so I settled the cat down and resolved to pick up the hunt for the owner the next day.

This cat had been one of several being fed by an elderly lady, but he had been aggressive to the other stray cats that she was feeding so she wanted him taken away – she had been feeding him for some six or seven months! She had seen the collar, but it never occurred to her to ring the owner's number!

The next day I began my attempts to locate an owner, and after several telephone calls I established that the name of this beautiful pedigree was no less than *Pork Pie!* He had gone missing some six or seven months earlier, just before Christmas, and his owners had spent a miserable holiday season believing him to be dead. They had done all the right things to try and find him, such as putting up posters, newspaper adverts and contacting all the lost and found register keepers, but it was all to no avail. Soon after Christmas they were going to move into a new house and even then they informed everyone they had spoken to previously and gave them their new contact details in case Pork Pie was found. After five months they gave up hope of ever finding him and bought a pair of Burmese kittens, and guess what? They could no longer have Pork Pie back and were trying to find him a new home – could I look after him in the meantime?

Pork Pie – or Porky, as he became known – was an experience I shall never forget. He wanted to be top cat in a house where the pecking order had already been established, and he was definitely the new boy on the block, but it didn't stop this very determined cat from trying to get to the top!

I had an ornamental wrought iron balcony at one end of my lounge, and on hot summer evenings the cats liked to lie on the thick bars, allowing any breeze to flow around keeping them cool. William was particularly fond of this balcony, and he was lying there one evening minding his own business when Porky decided that he wanted to sit out there too, but he didn't want to share it, so he howled at William quite aggressively to try and make him move. Nothing happened, so he howled again. And again. And again. William had grown into a big, fat lump of a cat that never rushed into doing anything. He sat solidly on his spot on the balcony while Porky continued to howl at him. Eventually it registered in William's brain that these howls were directed at him, and his head turned slightly to look at Porky. He blinked a couple of times and then his head moved back to its previous position – he hadn't moved an inch! Pork Pie learned a lesson that evening: that in our house he had to share things, and with a few sighs and whines he too sat out on the balcony to keep William company.

An almighty crash rocked the house as the curtains and the railing came away from the bedroom window after Porky had tried to climb the curtains. I told him off in a very loud voice, and immediately he hid under the bed; Porky did not like being told off by me! I went back downstairs having repaired the damage as best I could, and as I sat in the armchair I could see, out of the corner of my eye, that Porky was creeping down the stairs very cautiously. As he got to the bottom step, he peered round the corner of the wall and looked at me.

'Grr! You naughty boy!' I said, in what I hoped was my most reprimanding voice. It appeared to work, as he turned tail and fled back upstairs only to repeat the performance five minutes or so later. Eventually he won the battle of wills, and after several attempts to see whether I had forgiven him, I relented and found myself saying, 'Oh, come on then.'

He needed no more encouragement and rushed over to sit on my knee, probably thinking that he had got away with his misdemeanour yet again.

Porky was quite dominant and aggressive towards the other cats at times in his internal struggle to fulfil his need to be top cat, but he came unstuck one day with the smallest cat in the house…

One Sunday he had been particularly nasty to most of the cats in the house and despite being chastised by me on several occasions he kept up his relentless attempts to dominate them all. I suddenly heard a howl from the hallway and rushed down in time to see Trouble – who had not made her fateful decision to go outside at this point – walloping Porky with some ferocity, so much so that he rushed upstairs with his tail between his back legs and a large scratch on his nose; Trouble had his utmost respect from that moment onwards, but he still carried on with his assaults on the other cats.

Porky was still wearing the scar following his little set-to with Trouble when I heard that a new home had been found for him and arrangements were made for him to be collected. I was sorry to see him going into the cat basket, as I had grown quite fond of him, but for the sake of restoring peace and harmony in my home I had to let him go, and as the car drove away I started to repair all the damage this pedigree cat had done to my house!

...And Nobby the Hero

Just before Christmas one year there was just one cat left at the vet's needing a foster place, and with fosterers either away visiting families or with guests staying for the holiday period, I volunteered to look after the cat on the proviso that as soon as there was a space he would be moved on. This was a black-and-white adult male of about nine years old, and I envisaged spending the holiday season breaking up fights for male supremacy between the silly boys in my house and this new lodger.

However, Nobby came and it was almost as though he had never lived anywhere else. No one took any notice of him, other than a cursory sniff to welcome him to the house. He was a handsome cat with a very commanding air about him. I used to imagine him, in a previous life, as a colonel of the troops, boldly leading his men into battle from the front.

Nobby's owner was a long-distance lorry driver and, so the story goes, he spent long periods of time away from home and he was finding it more and more difficult to get anyone to feed the cat, and the neighbours were also complaining that the cat howled when he was left on his own. I soon discovered that the latter part of this story was true, at least; Nobby *was* a howler if he thought he was on his own – especially at night. He would come into my bedroom and stand with his two paws on the edge of my bed and howl until I woke up and stroked him, reassuring him that I was still here and everything was okay. After several sleepless nights, I was beginning to look forward to the day when he was moved to another fosterer.

One night I was awoken by Nobby howling frantically. I dragged myself out of bed and tried to calm him down. I noticed that I had left a light on downstairs, and having quietened Nobby, I went downstairs to switch the light off, only to find out that I had been burgled whilst I was asleep. Nobby must have been trying to alert me to the fact that there were intruders downstairs. I discovered later that all the other brave male cats in the house had converged on the bedroom for safety!

I often wonder what the burglars must have thought when they heard him howl, and I believe that their haul would have been greater had I remained asleep. So, Nobby joined the family on a permanent basis – how could I have let him go somewhere else after such a show of bravery? I will always think of him as my hero.

He was a lovely, affectionate old cat who would put his paws up around my neck and purr loudly in my ear. He liked to sleep on his blanket on top of the work surface in the kitchen, and if I had removed his blanket to wash it and forgotten to put another in its place, he would sit in the middle of the kitchen floor and howl until I realised my misdemeanour and quickly found another clean blanket for him to sleep on. He would grizzle his chastisements as he kneaded the new blanket before settling down to sleep.

Nobby's stay with me was all too short; his kidneys stopped functioning all of a sudden. He had shown no signs of being in pain or ill, and the first inkling I had was when his bladder gave way as he sat on my knee for his evening cuddle. I rushed him to the vet the next morning and he was put on a drip, but within two days he was put to sleep as there was nothing the vet could do to prolong his life. I vowed there and then, in his memory, to promote the plight of the older cats who are never given the chance of a new home if there is a kitten or young cat available. The pleasure they can give their new owners is immeasurable – as Nobby proved to me.

Several weeks later I was awoken by a familiar sound – Nobby was howling. As I turned over in bed there he was as usual, two front feet on the side of my bed, looking at me intently. He howled again and before I fell back into a deep sleep, I managed to say, 'Hello, Nobby. Don't worry, I'm here. Now go back to sleep.'

When I awoke the next morning, I pondered over Nobby's visit. Was it just a dream, or had I really had a visit from another realm?

Seventy-five per cent of me believes that I *did* wake up that night and see him at the side of my bed; twenty-five per cent of me thinks it was just a dream. Whichever the case may be, I believe wholeheartedly that Nobby actually *did* pay me one last visit that night – just to let me know that he was all right and would continue to watch over me until we are reunited at Rainbow Bridge.

Chapter Sixteen

Minnie Mouse

I WAS ASKED TO DELIVER A COUPLE OF CAT BASKETS TO a girl who lived not very far away from me as she was going to take her cats to the vet to be neutered and then they were going to go to a sanctuary not far from us. As I stood on her doorstep listening to her propose that her son would take the cats to the vet on his pedal bike, my attention was drawn to a clip-clop noise on the lino, and as I looked, coming towards me was a tiny little black cat with funny little tipped ears and a pointed face.

'Oh, isn't she sweet!' I said, scooping the tiny little thing up into my arms. As I looked at her I followed up with, 'There's something wrong with her mouth.'

'Is there?' the girl replied. 'I've never noticed. She was the runt of the litter and we had to hand rear her – maybe that has something to do with it.'

My mind was racing and I arranged with the girl that I would come down the next morning and collect the cats to take them to the vet in my car rather than subjecting them to being dangled over handlebars on her son's bike. I couldn't stop thinking about the dear little cat all evening, and worried about the idea of her being taken to a sanctuary, no matter how good it might be.

The next morning I collected the cats and took them to the vet. As I entered the surgery I found myself saying, 'I'm keeping this cat, so I want her spayed if she is old enough, and her first injection done. I will be back to collect her later.'

When I returned that afternoon, Laura the vet met me.

'I know why you want this one; she's a real oddity,' she said. 'I haven't spayed her yet, as I think we should wait a little longer to see if she grows some more. She's got an undershot jaw and loads of teeth – she is quite cute though. I've got her vaccination card here. What are you going to call her?'

I'd given this some considerable thought during the day. 'Mouse,' I said.

A chorus of voices met my ears. 'You can't call a cat *Mouse*!'

I was browbeaten, so the unanimous decision was that she would be called Minnie Mouse, but I noticed that on her vaccination card only the name Minnie appeared, and so she was christened.

Minnie quickly discovered all the important things that she needed to know about her new home, and these included the sort of menu she would be expected to eat. She learned that the fridge contained lots of tasty morsels of chicken and turkey, both of which remain her absolute favourite form of food to this day. Being small, if I left the fridge door ajar, I would turn around to find Minnie inside sniffing all the packages, looking for what was rightfully hers. She used to sleep on top of the microwave, but I had to put a stop to that because she rolled over and fell off so many times that I thought she might do herself an injury. Then she moved to sleeping on top of the TV during the day and my pillow on the bed at night; I would often wake up to the sound of Minnie doing her ablutions in the middle of the night, and sometimes my face would come in for a good clean – not something I would recommend for a good night's sleep!

Minnie's little mouth was crammed full of two rows of teeth that caused very severe gum infections. By this time our vet was Sandra, and she recommended taking out Minnie's teeth.

'Don't take out the front teeth,' I pleaded. 'Minnie has such problems picking up food, and with no front teeth she won't manage at all.'

The day came and Minnie underwent her operation. When I went to pick her up Sandra said, 'Everything went better than I had expected and here's a present for you.' She presented me with a plastic bag containing all Minnie's removed teeth. 'I thought you might want to put them under her pillow for the tooth fairy tonight!'

Why is it that I always seem to have a vet with an ambition to become a comedian? After a few days on antibiotics and with plenty of soft chicken to eat, Minnie was back to her normal self and was even eating biscuits. She still had all her front teeth, although another thing we noticed was that her top jaw was also slightly out of line – just another thing that made her special.

Minnie was quite fond of Nobby and liked to curl up with him on his blanket at the end of the work surface in the kitchen. I'm not sure that Nobby was so keen, as Minnie was – and still is – a fidget. He would groan and meow as she pushed and shoved him into position around her tiny frame before they could both curl up to sleep together.

Arthur she saw as her playmate and they would rush around the room after a small green and red striped ball like a couple of football hooligans. The ball would crash against the skirting boards and then ricochet across the room with these two black rockets following – they'd play for ages!

Despite her size, Minnie was no shrinking violet and when the boys in the house decided to have a period of rough play, there in the middle of these extremely large males would be Minnie being thrown in the air, sat on and rolled over. At first I was worried that she might get hurt, but the one advantage that she had was her size, and if things got too hot for her to handle she would scoot off out of trouble and hide under a chair.

We had a big black-and-white cat who used to invade the cat flap from time to time, and on one of his sorties into the kitchen he was scared off by five cats: William, Arthur, George and Ziggy rushed out through the cat flap and followed the invader down the garden. Out in front of her 'brothers' was Minnie, chasing him away. Pixie, who was easily the scariest of the cats, trailed some way behind on this occasion.

Minnie had another 'little problem' – constipation. She needed regular help to ease this problem, and liquid paraffin was just one of the things that I had to keep in the cat medicine chest to help ease her difficulties – until, that is, we discovered that evaporated milk (or 'vappy' to us) had the same effect and was much more pleasant to take. Friends who wanted to buy a treat for Minnie would quietly hand me a tin of evaporated milk. 'For Minnie's little problem,' they would whisper.

The problem was probably worse because Minnie loved chicken, which was used to bind cats with the reverse problem, so I started to give her a tiny drop of vappy after her chicken dinner, and thereafter Minnie expected her 'pudding' every time she had dinner. She could tell the time, too; she knew that she always had supper before bedtime, and if I happened to be a little late in going to bed, Minnie would start to pace the floor between my chair and the kitchen door as if trying to hint that I really should be sorting out her food. As soon as I got up she would run ahead of me and jump up on the kitchen work surface just above the fridge to wait for her favourite food to be taken out and put into her supper bowl.

In many ways, Minnie took over from dear departed Posey as my number one confidante. As I talked to her she would put on a very serious expression as though she were trying to understand what it was that I was saying to her. Her paw would come up and pat my face very gently as though she were offering some form of consolation while she studied my mouth and the words that were coming from my lips. There are times now when I believe that she actually does understand what I am saying.

I could have re-homed Minnie a dozen times over – and there were times when I even considered it momentarily, as she could be quite naughty, especially when she didn't get her own way over something or when she felt that I was ignoring her. However, she was then – and still is – very endearing, and when she lies on her back in my arms with one paw outstretched for me to blow butterfly kisses on her pads, I know I could never part with her.

Chapter Seventeen

Katy, Queen of the Car Park!

THE BITING WIND CAUSED ME TO SHIVER AND REMINDED me of the tale of woe that had brought me to this private car park on this cold Sunday afternoon. David had to leave his rented flat because the council said it was not habitable and the private landlord refused to do any repairs. He had five semi-feral, un-neutered cats – one a pregnant queen – and he could not take them with him to his new bedsit; enter one out of practise but determined trapper!

Now the story becomes confusing, because David wasn't very imaginative when it came to naming his cats – especially the females. The males were quite easy as he called them Clifford, Foreman and Lucky. However, the two females were Katy Number One and Katy Number Two (not to be confused with my own dear Katie).

The first cat to be caught was tabby and white: Katy Number Two – a tiny replica of her mother, Katy Number One. She went into the manual trap quite easily on the first day. David managed to force Clifford, one of the three males, into a basket the next day, and a day or so later Foreman walked into one of the traps and David, who was kneeling by the side of the trap, managed to simply shut the door behind him. Lucky, the other male was caught several weeks later. Each time a cat was caught David would be in tears. 'This is killing me,' he would sob. 'I do love them – they will be all right, won't they? They will stay together, won't they?'

I felt very sorry for him, but equally I was annoyed that

he had not had the sense to have the cats neutered or to handle them, which would have made catching them so much easier; he had just fed them and loved them.

Katy Number One was our big problem. She was noticeably pregnant and had taken up residence in a nearby churchyard and the car park belonging to a block of flats. The car park was surrounded by flats and houses and, in full view of all the residents, we began our campaign to catch Katy Number One.

The first day we tried a manual trap in the hopes that she would go in to eat the food when encouraged by David. Then he would be able to shut the door behind her. It had worked with Foreman, but Katy was shrewd! As we tried time and time again to get her into the trap I was aware of net curtains twitching at the windows of the flats.

The cat was really enjoying all the attention, and she rubbed herself all over the outside of the trap and David, whilst ignoring the food offered to her. We gave up for the first evening and arranged to meet the next day. I decided to try the automatic trap and baited it with pilchards in tomato sauce – guaranteed to make a cat's mouth water!

Katy came running to greet us with her tail held high. 'Hello, you funny people,' she seemed to say. 'What games do you want to play tonight?'

She went right up to the trap and then proceeded to sniff her way around the outside. We held our breath as she waltzed into the trap and stopped with her front paws just on the edge of the metal plate that she was supposed to stand on to trigger the closure of the door behind her. Her head stretched over the footplate and she picked up a bit of the pilchard in her mouth and carried it outside the trap where she proceeded to eat it. She did this again and again – just to show off, I'm sure! The net curtains were twitching again and several people found very weak excuses to come into the car park for a better view. I thought we might as well call it a day and come back the next night.

I got to the car park early and David was late, so I had a wander around and saw Katy under the bushes in a small lawned garden. I called her and to my amazement she jumped up on the low brick wall surrounding the garden, tail upright and waving. 'Hello,' she seemed to say. 'I wondered if you'd be back. It's so nice to have company. Will we be playing games again?'

She kept far enough away to stop me making a grab for her scruff and bundling her into a basket, so I set the trap again. Katy went through her normal ritual of making love to the trap and, as David arrived, she looked to make sure that her entire audience was watching and then she tripped into the trap, stopped before the footplate and grabbed for the food. We gave up that night as well and settled our sights on the next evening and that was Friday, the last day of the week. This time I gave her a choice and put two traps out.

She looked at the manual one on all sides and then looked at me. 'If you think I am going in that one, you are frightfully mistaken!' her face seemed to say. Then she looked at the automatic trap from all angles – she recognised this one and this was a game that she knew how to play like a professional. She went in and out several times as if trying to prove how clever she was and how stupid we were. The net curtains were at it again! Frustrated and tired, I arranged to meet David on Monday (I thought we both needed a weekend to recover) for another attempt at capturing this little madam whose waistline was expanding almost daily – if we didn't catch her soon, we would have kittens to try and find as well.

My neighbours were entering into the spirit of things too, and every time they saw me load up the car with traps they would ask about the events of the previous day's attempts at catching her; I dreaded arriving home having failed once again – especially when I had to admit being outsmarted by a cat!

I talked my problem over with other trappers who had more experience than I did, and they came up with some ideas that might help, like putting a sheet of newspaper over the footplate so that Katy couldn't see it and having a deep bowl to put the food in so that she had to put her head in and lift the food out. I decided that I would go back on Sunday armed with the specially modified trap and without David, whose tears and protestations of love for the cat were beginning to be a little irritating; I was beginning to believe that he was quite happy for her to remain in the car park and have me going over to keep both of them company forever.

Sunday came, and armed with a flask of coffee, some nibbles and a specially adapted trap, I set off alone to catch Katy – who by now saw me as a friend! I arrived at the site during the late afternoon; we usually came at about six o'clock in the evening to feed her and play with her. As I was setting the trap in the car park, an elderly lady and her grandson came over to me. 'Are you looking for the cat?' she asked. 'Well, I've just seen her down there,' she said, pointing to the other end of the short road.

I asked her if she was sure and told her that I was looking for a pregnant tabby-and-white cat. She assured me that she had seen the cat in the direction in which she was pointing, so I picked up the trap and trudged down the road, only to find that the cat in question was a nice little tortie quietly going about her business in her own front garden.

I returned to the car park and set the trap before returning to wait in my car. After what seemed like an eternity, I caught site of Katy coming from the direction of the churchyard and across the car park. She meandered over towards the trap, which was out of my sight behind a low brick wall. I quietly got out of my car and went towards the wall to get a clearer view. She had actually moved away from the trap and was sitting under a parked car, and as I watched she got up, sniffed the trap and then walked towards the entrance of the car park just near where I was standing watching her.

She first looked up the road, away from me, and then she looked down the road towards me. 'Oh, there you are,' she seemed to say. 'I thought I was going to have to play by myself, and that's no fun!' Apparently happy that she had an audience, she wandered back into the car park.

I waited patiently until I suddenly heard the noise of the metal door on the trap shutting. I grabbed a towel to throw over the trap and, praying that I had caught Katy and not some other poor cat, I shot into the car park – it was Katy! I picked up the trap and its contents and went to put them in the car, and as I did so the old lady and her grandson appeared at my shoulder.

'Did you catch her?' she asked, to which I nodded, smugly.

'You've been ever so patient; I said to my daughter, that lady has been ever so patient all week.'

After uttering assurances that nothing nasty was going to happen to the cat and that she would be allowed to have her kittens in safety, I got in the car and drove off – never to return, hopefully. I had seen enough of that car park to last me a lifetime.

Katy Number Two was found a home with some nice people who wanted a playmate for their own young cat. Clifford, Foreman and Lucky were neutered, micro-chipped, vaccinated and offered a home on a farm of twenty-five acres where they would be treated as house cats rather than farm cats and would be able to enjoy the country air and country pursuits whilst there would always be someone human around to make sure they were fit and healthy.

What about Katy Number One? Well, Katy had her kittens a week after she was caught – there were four of them and they were all found nice new homes to grow up in. Katy herself was spayed, micro-chipped and vaccinated, and happily she was offered a home with Foreman, Clifford and Lucky on the farm, so you can think of her – as I shall – enjoying the country life in the company of the cats she had grown up with. I admit that I had grown quite fond of that cheeky little cat during the course of the week when she and I became friends whilst playing the trapping games!

Chapter Eighteen

Until We Meet Again

I COULD NEVER HAVE IMAGINED THE PATHWAY MY LIFE would be following on that day, all those years ago, when I first collected Tabatha from the RSPCA sanctuary. At that time I believe that I thought that the RSPCA was the only animal welfare charity in existence, whereas now I am aware of the hundreds of charities, both large and small, all dedicated to helping animals that are suffering cruelty and neglect at the hands of humans.

Fifteen years have passed since I wrote that first fateful letter offering my help to the Cats Protection League, and each day of those years has been spent trying to make life better for one cat or another – and there are many other volunteers throughout the country who are equally devoted to trying to make that little bit of difference to the lives of cats, kittens and other animals in distress.

Having been brought up from childhood with an assortment of rabbits, cats, dogs, budgies, canaries, pigeons, ducks, chickens and the odd guinea pig or two, I cannot imagine a life without animals, and I know that my home will always be full of cats. Some of the ones that you have now become acquainted with still share my life, and there have been countless others that I hope I have helped along the pathway to a happier future.

I personally have to thank all the cats – past, present and future – for enhancing my life beyond any previous recognition and filling it with love and friendship, both feline and human. They have encouraged me to rediscover and recognise talents such as writing, knitting, sewing, painting and craft work – all used to raise funds to help pay for the essential needs of a cat in distress.

I genuinely look forward to the day when, at Rainbow Bridge, I am reunited with all those cats that have shared my life and given me their unconditional love, and whom I miss to this very day, particularly Tabatha, Ziggy, Posey, Daisy and Oliver – not forgetting Thomas, who surely was the catalyst that helped me to discover the reason for my own existence.

Made in the USA
San Bernardino, CA
03 February 2017